*Ricarda B. Bouncken*
*Sungsoo Pyo*
*Editors*

# Knowledge Management in Hospitality and Tourism

*Knowledge Management in Hospitality and Tourism* has been co-published simultaneously as *Journal of Quality Assurance in Hospitality & Tourism*, Volume 3, Numbers 3/4 2002.

*Pre-publication REVIEWS, COMMENTARIES, EVALUATIONS . . .*

"THE FIRST OF ITS KIND. . . . A thought-provoking perspective on ways to move hospitality and tourism forward in this knowledge-driven world."

**Billy Bai, PhD**
*Assistant Professor
Tourism & Convention
Administration Department
William F. Harrah College
of Hotel Administration
University of Nevada at Las Vegas*

THHP
The Haworth Hospitality Press

# Knowledge Management in Hospitality and Tourism

*Knowledge Management in Hospitality and Tourism* has been co-published simultaneously as *Journal of Quality Assurance in Hospitality & Tourism,* Volume 3, Numbers 3/4 2002.

# The *Journal of Quality Assurance in Hospitality & Tourism*™ Monographic "Separates"

Executive Editor: Sungsoo Pyo

Below is a list of "separates," which in serials librarianship means a special issue simultaneously published as a special journal issue or double-issue *and* as a "separate" hardbound monograph. (This is a format which we also call a "DocuSerial.")

"Separates" are published because specialized libraries or professionals may wish to purchase a specific thematic issue by itself in a format which can be separately cataloged and shelved, as opposed to purchasing the journal on an on-going basis. Faculty members may also more easily consider a "separate" for classroom adoption.

"Separates" are carefully classified separately with the major book jobbers so that the journal tie-in can be noted on new book order slips to avoid duplicate purchasing.

You may wish to visit Haworth's website at . . .

## http://www.HaworthPress.com

. . . to search our online catalog for complete tables of contents of these separates and related publications.

You may also call 1-800-HAWORTH (outside US/Canada: 607-722-5857), or Fax 1-800-895-0582 (outside US/Canada: 607-771-0012), or e-mail at:

## docdelivery@haworthpress.com

---

*Knowledge Management in Hospitality and Tourism,* edited by Ricarda B. Bouncken and Sungsoo Pyo (Vol. 3, No. 3/4, 2002). *"Of great value. . . Introduces the concepts associated with knowledge management and provides examples of these concepts through case studies and unique real-world applications. . . . A lot of great information on a fascinating topic. . . ." (Cary C. Countryman, PhD, CHE, CHTP, Director, Technology Research and Education Center, Conrad N. Hilton College of Hotel and Restaurant Management)*

*Benchmarks in Hospitality and Tourism,* edited by Sungsoo Pyo (Vol. 2, No. 3/4, 2001). *"A handy single volume that clearly explains the principles and current thinking about benchmarking, plus useful insights on how the techniques can be converted into profitable business operations. Includes conceptual, practical, and operational (or 'how-it-is-done') chapters." (Chris Ryan, PhD, MEd, MPhil, BSc (Econ) Hons, Professor of Tourism, The University of Waikato, Hamilton, New Zealand)*

# Knowledge Management in Hospitality and Tourism

Ricarda B. Bouncken
Sungsoo Pyo
Editors

*Knowledge Management in Hospitality and Tourism* has been co-published simultaneously as *Journal of Quality Assurance in Hospitality & Tourism,* Volume 3, Numbers 3/4 2002.

The Haworth Hospitality Press
An Imprint of
The Haworth Press, Inc.
New York • London • Oxford

Published by

The Haworth Hospitality Press®, 10 Alice Street, Binghamton, NY 13904-1580 USA

The Haworth Hospitality Press® is an imprint of The Haworth Press, Inc., 10 Alice Street, Binghamton, NY 13904-1580 USA.

*Knowledge Management in Hospitality and Tourism* has been co-published simultaneously as *Journal of Quality Assurance in Hospitality & Tourism,* Volume 3, Numbers 3/4 2002.

The development, preparation, and publication of this work has been undertaken with great care. However, the publisher, employees, editors, and agents of The Haworth Press and all imprints of The Haworth Press, Inc., including The Haworth Medical Press® and Pharmaceutical Products Press®, are not responsible for any errors contained herein or for consequences that may ensue from use of materials or information contained in this work. Opinions expressed by the author(s) are not necessarily those of The Haworth Press, Inc. With regard to case studies, identities and circumstances of individuals discussed herein have been changed to protect confidentiality. Any resemblance to actual persons, living or dead, is entirely coincidental.

Cover design by Marylouise Doyle

**Library of Congress Cataloging-in-Publication Data**

Knowledge management in hospitality and tourism / Ricarda B. Bouncken, Sungsoo Pyo, editors.
    p. cm.
"Knowledge management in hospitality and tourism has been co-published simultaneously as Journal of quality assurance in hospitality & tourism, volume 3, numbers 3/4 2002."
Includes bibliographical references and index.
    ISBN 0-7890-2146-3–ISBN 0-7890-2147-1
1. Hospitality industry–Management. 2. Tourism–Management. 3. Knowledge management. I. Bouncken, Ricarda B. II. Pyo, Sungsoo. III. Journal of quality assurance in hospitality & tourism.

TX911.3.M27K62 2003
647.94'068–dc21

2003005572

# Indexing, Abstracting & Website/Internet Coverage

This section provides you with a list of major indexing & abstracting services. That is to say, each service began covering this periodical during the year noted in the right column. Most Websites which are listed below have indicated that they will either post, disseminate, compile, archive, cite or alert their own Website users with research-based content from this work. (This list is as current as the copyright date of this publication.)

Abstracting, Website/Indexing Coverage . . . . . . . . . Year When Coverage Began

- **CIRET (Centre International de Recherches et d'Etudes Touristiques). Computerized Touristique & General Bibliography <www.ciret-tourism.com>** . . . . . . . . . . . . . . . . . 2000

- **CNPIEC Reference Guide: Chinese National Directory of Foreign Periodicals** . . . . . . . . . . . . . . . . . . . . . . . . . . . . . . 2000

- **INSPEC <www.iee.org.uk/publish/>** . . . . . . . . . . . . . . . . . . . . . . 2000

- **Leisure, Recreation & Tourism Abstracts (c/o CAB Intl/CAB ACCESS) <www.cabi.org>** . . . . . . . . . . . 2000

- **Management & Marketing Abstracts** . . . . . . . . . . . . . . . . . . . . . . 2000

- **South African Assn for Food Science & Technology (SAAFOST)** . . . . . . . . . . . . . . . . . . . . . . . . . . . . . . . . . . . . . 2000

- **TOURISM: an international interdisciplinary journal** . . . . . . . . . 2000

(continued)

*Special Bibliographic Notes related to special journal issues (separates) and indexing/abstracting:*

- indexing/abstracting services in this list will also cover material in any "separate" that is co-published simultaneously with Haworth's special thematic journal issue or DocuSerial. Indexing/abstracting usually covers material at the article/chapter level.
- monographic co-editions are intended for either non-subscribers or libraries which intend to purchase a second copy for their circulating collections.
- monographic co-editions are reported to all jobbers/wholesalers/approval plans. The source journal is listed as the "series" to assist the prevention of duplicate purchasing in the same manner utilized for books-in-series.
- to facilitate user/access services all indexing/abstracting services are encouraged to utilize the co-indexing entry note indicated at the bottom of the first page of each article/chapter/contribution.
- this is intended to assist a library user of any reference tool (whether print, electronic, online, or CD-ROM) to locate the monographic version if the library has purchased this version but not a subscription to the source journal.
- individual articles/chapters in any Haworth publication are also available through the Haworth Document Delivery Service (HDDS).

# Knowledge Management in Hospitality and Tourism

## CONTENTS

# ABOUT THE EDITORS

**Ricarda B. Bouncken, Prof., Dr., oec, habil, Guest Editor,** is Chair for Planning and Innovation Management, Brandenburg University of Technology Cottbus, Germany. Dr. Bouncken is the winner of eight research awards and author of over 38 publications, many of them in refereed German and international journals. She is an active member of the Strategic Management Society, the Academy of Management, and the Academy of International Business. Dr. Bouncken's research interests include organizational theory, strategic management, service management, knowledge management, competencies, innovation, and external collaboration.

**Sungsoo Pyo, PhD,** is Professor in the Department of Tourism Management at Kyonggi University in Seoul, Korea, and the editor of the *Journal of Quality Assurance in Hospitality & Tourism* (Haworth). He is the author or co-author of five books and over 40 professional articles and has presented numerous papers at seminars. Dr. Pyo is on the editorial boards of five journals, including the *Journal of Travel & Tourism Marketing* and *Tourism Analysis.* He is President of Tourism Systems and Quality Management Research Association in Korea, and the editor of the *Journal of Tourism Systems and Quality Management,* published by the Association. In addition, he is the recipient of the Sosung Award for Academic Excellence, awarded by the President of Kyonggi University (1997) and the Outstanding Service Award from the International Management Development Association at the Sixth Annual IMDA World Business Congress (1997). Dr. Pyo's current research interests include destination marketing engineering, quantitative analysis and TQM for destination management. Dr. Pyo is a member of AIEST–the International Association of Scientific Experts in Tourism.

# INTRODUCTION

# Achieving Competitiveness
# Through Knowledge Management

Ricarda B. Bouncken
Sungsoo Pyo

**SUMMARY.** Effective knowledge management contributes in establishing competitive advantages over competitors in the hospitality and tourism industry. Reuse of already proven knowledge and readiness of knowledge to use are the major benefits of knowledge management. This paper introduces views of editors about knowledge management and dis-

Ricarda B. Bouncken is Chair for Planning and Innovation Management, Brandenburg University of Technology Cottbus, Erich-Weinert-Str. 1, 03044 Cottbus, Germany (E-mail: bouncken@tu.cottbus.de).

Sungsoo Pyo is Professor, Kyonggi University, Republic of Korea, and Visiting Scholar, Department of Leisure Studies, University of Illinois, 1206 S. 4th Street, 104 Huff Hall, Champaign, IL 61820 USA (E-mail: pyos@chollian.net).

[Haworth co-indexing entry note]: "Achieving Competitiveness Through Knowledge Management." Bouncken, Ricarda B., and Sungsoo Pyo. Co-published simultaneously in *Journal of Quality Assurance in Hospitality & Tourism* (The Haworth Hospitality Press, an imprint of The Haworth Press, Inc.) Vol. 3, No. 3/4, 2002, pp. 1-4; and: *Knowledge Management in Hospitality and Tourism* (ed: Ricarda B. Bouncken and Sungsoo Pyo) The Haworth Hospitality Press, an imprint of The Haworth Press, Inc., 2002, pp. 1-4. Single or multiple copies of this article are available for a fee from The Haworth Document Delivery Service [1-800-HAWORTH, 9:00 a.m. - 5:00 p.m. (EST). E-mail address: docdelivery@haworthpress.com].

10.1300/J162v03n03_01

cusses its possible applications, in addition to the papers included in this volume. *[Article copies available for a fee from The Haworth Document Delivery Service: 1-800-HAWORTH. E-mail address: <docdelivery@haworthpress. com> Website: <http://www.HaworthPress.com> © 2002 by The Haworth Press, Inc. All rights reserved.]*

**KEYWORDS.** Knowledge management, tourism, hospitality, reuse of knowledge

Core of knowledge management involves acquisition, explication, and communication of mission-specific professional expertise in a manner that is focused and relevant to an organizational participant who receives the communication (King, 1999: 70). Research on knowledge management has attracted increasing interest in the past years, which is indicated by a growing number of articles and management tools. A large number of articles have discussed the theoretical basis of knowledge or stressed the importance of knowledge in firms.

Knowledge management contributes to effective operations and establishes competitive advantages over competitors in the hospitality and tourism industry. When the proven knowledge during the field operations is re-used, knowledge developed during various formal and informal procedures can be incorporated in operations (Pyo, Uysal and Chang, 2002). As a result, duplication of research can be avoided, the cost of research and development is reduced, and effectiveness of operations is increased. Recognizing this fact, reuse of already developed knowledge is awarded in six sigma practices.

Knowledge is ready to be used as a result of knowledge management. This is a drastic change from the traditional practice that searches and develops knowledge after recognizing its need. Knowledge management provides knowledge in hand in advance, in anticipation of the knowledge use (Pyo, Uysal and Chang, 2002). When the knowledge is in hand, the speed of operations improves greatly by eliminating knowledge searching time. When the knowledge is based on internal team cooperation, copying the competitive advantage by the competitors can be very difficult.

Although tourism and hospitality, with their geographically dispersed units, can profit from an enhanced knowledge management system, only a small number of firms have implemented knowledge management up till now. A recent empirical study shows that although managers in many hotels consider knowledge management and information transfer to be relevant concepts, they report being confronted with too many and unclear knowledge management strategies, activities and implementation techniques. As a result, they are not sufficiently familiar with knowledge management and reject implementing knowledge management. This special issue will increase the understanding of the concepts and will aid the implementation of knowledge management in hospitality and tourism.

In this special issue, six articles are included. The articles deepen specific topics of knowledge management and show examples and cases of knowledge management, and the theme is well reflected in the articles altogether. The first paper describes mostly mental and conceptual aspects of knowledge management. The next two articles are theoretical and also include practical considerations in hospitality and airlines. The next papers include software application developments in knowledge management in general, in hospitality and tourism and cross-border destination management. The final paper deals with database marketing with data mining and knowledge discovery.

Kahle introduces the concept of mental models into tourism. Mental models can be understood as landscape of a persons' concepts and their interrelations. They are strongly influenced by individual experiences and the socialization process. Mental models are fundamental for people's understanding of the world and their strategies to cope with the environment. In tourism, people are confronted with very dissimilar mental models. This helps to produce a high variety of ideas and concepts, but this variety can produce misunderstanding, mistrust and can lead to conflicts. Kahle argues that if people involved in tourism understand and internalize the concept of different mental models, they will develop lower degrees of mistrust and can operate more efficiently.

Bouncken introduces an integrated concept of knowledge management. This article describes knowledge management in hotels, presents case-studies and gives strategic advice and structural recommendations for its implementation. While developing theoretical concepts which underpin the theory, the article provides reflections about knowledge and analyzes different dimensions of knowledge management in hotels. Further, it presents major influences on strategic and structural aspects of knowledge management in hotels and suggests structures for the implementation of knowledge management.

Hattendorf develops a matrix that combines strategic operative aspects of knowledge management. He illustrates his concept according to requirements in the airline industry. The knowledge supply chain matrix allows the balancing of various aspects within knowledge management aspects. The knowledge supply chain matrix assesses four generic factors (strategy, structure, process, resources) that are aligned according to core processes within knowledge management. Hattendorf derives the knowledge supply chain matrix from a generic business model and shows the way to apply it within a knowledge management project in the airline industry.

Gronau explains an IT-based knowledge management system, which primarily helps to manage explicit knowledge. Gronau develops the idea of a Knowledge Café and introduces it to hospitality and tourism. This knowledge management system contains layers of sources, repositories, taxonomy, services, applications and user interfaces.

Pechlaner, Abfalter, and Raich explain issues in cross-border Destination Management. Their example of the new project "AlpNet" demonstrates how important cooperation and member-specific requirements are for tourism and other economic industries when establishing knowledge networks.

Finally, Cho and Leung discuss knowledge discovery techniques in database marketing for the tourism industry. Data mining deals with the complex task of extracting and managing any potential knowledge embedded inside databases. This paper introduces the common techniques in data mining, including decision tree classifiers, regression analysis, induction programming logic, and probabilistic rules. Suggestions are made about how these techniques can be used in order to improve the database marketing. By utilizing database marketing, a company can increase its competitiveness and build entry barriers for others.

Most of the papers in this volume are theoretical or conceptual and practical, rather than empirical. This tendency is due to the rather short history of research about knowledge management in hospitality and tourism. This volume will contribute not only to the understanding of knowledge management in hospitality and tourism, but also to the advancement in research methods and research areas.

## REFERENCES

King, William R. (1999). "Integrating Knowledge Management into IS Strategy," *Information Systems Management*, Vol. 16, No. 4, pp. 70-72.

Pyo, Sungsoo, Uysal, Muzaffer and Chang, Hyesook. (2002) "Knowledge Discovery in Database for Tourist destinations," *Journal of Travel Research*, Vol. 40, pp. 396-403.

# ARTICLES

# Implications of "New Economy" Traits for the Tourism Industry

## Egbert Kahle

SUMMARY. The tourism industry is a knowledge-based industry. The recent developments in information processing and knowledge production and transfer have implications for the processes and relations in the tourism industry. The main aspects are the change of the structure of transaction costs, the increasing importance of networks and the impact of the conditions of knowledge transfer on the inter-industrial relations. The concept of cognitive maps is used to explain the processes of information transfer. The overall result of the different aspects of the knowl-

Egbert Kahle is Dean of Faculty, University of Lueneburg, Scharnhorststr. 1, 21332 Lueneburg, Germany (E-mail: quass@uni-lueneburg.de). His research is concentrated in planning and organization, SMEs, change and risk management and decisions under uncertainty.

[Haworth co-indexing entry note]: "Implications of 'New Economy' Traits for the Tourism Industry." Kahle, Egbert. Co-published simultaneously in *Journal of Quality Assurance in Hospitality & Tourism* (The Haworth Hospitality Press, an imprint of The Haworth Press, Inc.) Vol. 3, No. 3/4, 2002, pp. 5-23; and: *Knowledge Management in Hospitality and Tourism* (ed: Ricarda B. Bouncken and Sungsoo Pyo) The Haworth Hospitality Press, an imprint of The Haworth Press, Inc., 2002, pp. 5-23. Single or multiple copies of this article are available for a fee from The Haworth Document Delivery Service [1-800-HAWORTH, 9:00 a.m. - 5:00 p.m. (EST). E-mail address: docdelivery@haworthpress.com].

10.1300/J162v03n03_02

edge orientation of the tourism industry is the importance of trust as the core instrument in this industry. *[Article copies available for a fee from The Haworth Document Delivery Service: 1-800-HAWORTH. E-mail address: <docdelivery@haworthpress.com> Website: <http://www.HaworthPress. com> © 2002 by The Haworth Press, Inc. All rights reserved.]*

**KEYWORDS.** Asymmetric information, attributes of knowledge production, cognitive maps, knowledge transfer, networks, organizational arrangements, transaction costs, trust

## KNOWLEDGE MANAGEMENT AND KNOWLEDGE INTENSITY IN THE TOURISM INDUSTRY

### Knowledge Intensity As a Core Attribute of Tourism

The travel industry or tourism industry is a very heterogeneous area of service production. The first denomination is used more for business travelers, whereas the second one is used for leisure traveling. Both will be included in the following discussions although the writer respects the great differences in the kinds of services required in each group. This is a complex field with different areas of production distributed in different countries and regions. The products and the processes of operation, which are used for the achievement of the resulting services, are related to different types of industries, but they have one common denominator: They are knowledge-based or knowledge-intensive service processes. The tourism system consists mainly of five areas, within which differing elements compete and co-operate with each other. These areas are (Bouncken, 2000: 91) the Agency, the Tour Operator, the Carrier, the In-Coming-System and the Hotel. There may be additional areas like Entertainment, Shopping and the like for the support of the travelers at the destination. The special attributes of the travel industry as a service process, the intangibility of the product and the simultaneity of production and consumption (Corsten, 1985: 173; Langeard, 1981: 233), have been discussed widely elsewhere (Bouncken, 2000: 91-93). The focus of this paper lies in the tourism service as a knowledge-based process, which is greatly influenced by the developments of information and communication technologies.

Within each of the main areas of tourism, there are a large number of participants as suppliers and purchasers of services, which partly cooperate and partly compete with each other. These cooperative and competitive relations are embedded in flows of knowledge and information. The elements of these systems are connected in various ways with others in the system, which results in quite different configurations of elements. Hence, we find many different forms of organizational arrangements for the coordination of the service process. These arrangements are changing or have the opportunity to change due to developments in information processing methods. One of the more important aspects concerning this development is the increasing use of networks as a form of organization, which tends to be an organizational form of its own beyond market and hierarchy (Fischer, 2001: 124-136; Gerum, 2001: 10) and not between them (Williamson, 1985: 751). In these networks, the main coordination mechanism is trust, whereas in markets it is contracts and in hierarchies the authority to issue instructions.

### The Main Features of "New Economy" and Knowledge Economy

The intensive use of knowledge in the process of service production and the vast amounts of information connected with the numerous and varying cooperative and competitive relations handled with modern IT-equipment put the tourism industry close to the New Economy, even though it is part of the Old Economy. The intensive use of knowledge or information is the main feature of all the New Economy industries (Kahle, 2002a: 175), so we may subsume the tourism industry here, because today this industry is in many ways knowledge-based. For these industries have been argued (Kelley, 1997: 140) that economic laws like "diminishing marginal growth of returns" or the theory of transaction costs are no longer valid. The actual development in the stock markets indicates some doubts to that and for further discussion we will look into the special attributes of knowledge as an economic good, especially its conditions of production and sale. These attributes are (Rode, 2001):

- The utility of knowledge in the process of knowledge transfer is dependent on the receiver (due to differences in the preferences, complementarity, the reflexivity of knowledge and to the co-production-problem).
- The transfer of knowledge is–in contrast to the transfer of information–very time-expensive (due to the limited lingual, psychological and pragmatic compatibility and to a limited speed of learning).

- The owner of knowledge can only with difficulties be protected against unlicensed proliferation and use of the knowledge (due to unlimited usefulness of the knowledge, minimal costs of reproduction and transport, and the impossibility of returning the given knowledge to the owner).

These attributes imply three different causal relations in the analysis of preparation and use of knowledge goods:

- The rapid increase, or more a jump, in the velocity of information transfer changes the structure of the transaction costs drastically. The consequences of "high velocity environments" for strategic decision processes have been discussed earlier (Bourgeois & Eisenhardt, 1988:816).
- The conditions of using knowledge induce a cost structure, where the variable costs are nearly dispensable and only the fixed costs are relevant for the strategic decisions. This is combined with the introduction of standards by the successful "First Mover."
- The "classic" framework of "simple" contracts in a market is no longer existent and the hierarchical structure of organizations is according to changing limits of time and space in the informational relations no longer relevant.

These three developments, which are discussed in detail in the next three sections, are accompanied by an increasing complexity of the structure of service and management relations, where the high velocity of the reactions induces within a short time dynamic, i.e., "time-lagged causal" effects. The great number of transactions per day, exchanging services, information and money, makes it possible that within short periods of time, very small variations in the transactions processes accumulate to big differences.

### The Impact of Change in the Structure of Transactions Costs

The change in the structure of the transactions costs has two different consequences for the tourism industry. The reduction of transaction costs in the pre-contract stage (preparation of contract) increases the number of possible partners. Instead of seeking scarce information about partners, we have today the situation of "information overload," where huge masses of information can be scanned by intelligent agents (Hecker, 1999: 41 and 137). Information about the possible partners is available for each of the elements in the system, the travelers, the agencies, the carriers, the hotels. Private travelers, tourists, may not have the IT-technology to scan all this information, but all professional travelers, the travel agencies, the carriers and most hotels will have access to this information. The result is that instead of a few selected market partners (Theisen, 1970) there are great numbers of them from which they can choose. This increase of potential partners, which provides for more freedom of choice and a wider variety of partners, is connected with greater anonymity of these partners, with the consequence that experience-based or trust-based goods and services are more difficult to evaluate. The services in the tourism industry are mostly experience- or trust-based (Bouncken, 2000: 89), and the problem of asymmetric information exists in the supplier-customer relations of these goods, which will be addressed further below. When the quality of the service is only assessable after some time or experience, questions such as the following are raised:

- What happens if the service doesn't meet the expectations or the conditions of the contract?
- Where and how are such problems dealt with?
- Is the service assessable at all, either ex ante or ex post?

Normally, these questions are answered by the rules and customs of the industry. But with the numerous new partners, there is no "custom of the industry," because they may come from different industries or countries. Hence, intercultural differences (Hofstede, 1993) and barriers may exist which must be overcome (Küsters, 1998; Kahle, 2002c). This shall be carried out with the concept of cognitive maps. Such cultural differences will be found when the services in the different parts of the tourism process are given in different countries. Different cultural standards are related to the four dimensions (Hofstede, 1982): "power distance," "uncertainty avoidance," "individualism" and "masculinity" which lead to different interpretations of given information. Even so, simple things like nodding the head means "Yes" in some cultures and "no" in others, and the traveler will have problems if he nods to a question and does not get correct answers. The same problems arise when staff members from different countries are working together in the same service production process, where the differences in contextuality of language (high context vs. low context) induce misinterpretations of information (Hall and Reed Hall, 1990).

As a result, we find that the reduction of transaction costs leads to an increase in the amount of information and to an increase of cultural diversity, which is to be expected in the increased number of possible contacts.

### The Impact of Knowledge Production Conditions

The special condition of knowledge production and sales is the other important aspect. Whereas the production and transfer of knowledge is quite expensive–due to the preference and complementarity differences of the users, the co-production problem, the limited learning speed and the limited compatibility of the knowledge transfer partners–the costs of transfer of information have decreased drastically. When knowledge is easily externalized (Nonaka et al., 1994) the transfer process of knowledge depends on the learning capacity of the information receiver and also on the matching of the relevant cognitive maps. The sender of the information can be a firm in one of the parts of the tourism industry or its employees that provide information about their services, prices, conditions and partners involved. The receivers are the potential travelers themselves or employees of the agencies, tour operators, carriers in the foregoing phases of the process. If they have similar cognitive maps on the core information, then they can understand the information very easily. If the maps don't match well, then the embedding process of the received information will need time and will result in changes of the underlying knowledge. For example, "The climate at the destination in April is quite fair and warm" will mean very different real temperatures if one is speaking about Helsinki, Kairo or Rangoon. So the receiver of the information must have a pre-information, what "quite fair and warm" is in this case.

Today, the process of knowledge transfer has emancipated from the information transfer process. Whereas in the past the information transfer process was characterized by the activities "hearing" or "reading" and "writing," which are accompanied partly by understanding the information and thereby creating knowledge in the receiving person, today by copying or by electronic exchange of data. These activities don't touch the receiver's cognitive map. Therefore, there is a great amount of information available in the tourism industry, but without the necessary cultural and technical context, it doesn't create knowledge in the receiver of the information.

Another aspect of the problem is the impression that the law of diminishing returns is no longer valid. This may be induced by the following argument: The information transfer processes themselves have very small variable costs–marginal above zero–therefore it seems that when the price is not zero, that there are increasing marginal returns since the situation is changed on the cost side.

Most important is the irrevocability of the knowledge transfer. Once the knowledge has been acquired by another person, it cannot be taken back. Therefore the validity of the "quid pro quo" must be secured by other measures than those applied to physical goods that can be returned. This implies that there is greater moral hazard in the knowledge transfer process than in other services rendered. The knowledge acquired by persons is not only irrevocable, but it is changed in the process of adaptation and embedding in the cognitive map. For the acquirers it becomes their own knowledge, which as their property gives them the right to use according to their own choice (Radetzki, 1999: 256).

These attributes of the knowledge transfer process imply that firms whose competitive advantage relies on a knowledge advantage should not externalize too much of their knowledge and share it with others, except if they are able to produce new knowledge as fast or faster than they give it away. This implies for the tourism industry that the knowledge about elements and relations in the five basic parts of tourism should not be made accessible to everybody, because it could be copied and allow competitors to match the offers of the firm.

### Trust as a Main Factor in Tourism Industry Relations

The third important aspect of the knowledge intensity in the tourism processes–implied by the two first aspects–is the increasing importance of trust in the relations between the acting elements (Bouncken, 2000). Trust as the expectation that the trusted will be able and willing to fulfill the positive expectation of the trustee is a social relationship. The trusted may be an individual, then we speak of personal trust, or an institution, where we speak of institutional trust (Luhmann, 1989). There is a third kind of trust, the ontological trust (Böhme, 1998), which means the reliance on one's own cognitive maps, built up by experience. The ability to give and take trust–to be trusted and to be a trustee–is an individual attribute and is acquired in the process of socialization (in the general meaning of Piaget, 1979: 88). The knowledge intensive services and relations in the tourism industry need trust, because the exchanged goods underlie asymmetric information. These trustful relations–either personal or institutional–can only be established over time. The high speed of the information transfer processes is compensated by the low speed of the trust building processes. Only within existing trustful relations will the advantages of the high speed information processes produce the economic gains expected from them.

Therefore the known and trusted partners will be the basis for the economic success in the tourism industry and trust as a part of the implicit knowledge (Polanyi, 1966) of persons and organizations will be a core competence in this industry. This is valid for the B2B relations in the tourism industry and applies too for travelers who don't want to be surprised by unexpected qualities of the services. For the travelers very often instead of personal experience the source of trust is the reputation of agencies, operators or carriers or the personal recommendation by trusted friends. The latter case could be called a "second order" trust, which is quite necessary in the tourism industry, because the travelers normally have no regular and much repeated relations with the travel agencies or the other partners in the tourism system.

## COGNITIVE MAPS IN THE APPREHENSION OF PROCESSES IN THE TOURISM INDUSTRY

### The Concept of Cognitive Maps

In the discussion of knowledge transfer the concept of cognitive maps plays an important role. We believe that the processes of construction or re-construction of reality in the individual mind and within organizations–where we have difficulties to localize physically the place of the mind–can be described and represented with the concept of cognitive maps or cause maps. Both words and concepts have been in use for more than twenty years (Taylor & Lerner, 1996: 260). This concept is used in different relations and levels of analysis, so we have to refer to four different concepts or views of cognitive maps.

In the first view–and it was the only one in the beginning and it is the basic view for all the other concepts–"cognitive map" is a metaphoric description of all the processes involved in obtaining, storing, retrieving and adapting knowledge and of the structure of knowledge, which is emerging and continuously varying. These processes and structures contain models of description, models of explication and decision models which initiate action (Kahle, 2001: 18). The analogy of "map" is quite limited, because the cognitive map contains much more than a normal map. It contains rules of observation, interpretation and action and often gives explanations. These mental processes and structures are the "real" or "original" cognitive map.

In the second meaning, cognitive maps are the pictures of these processes and structures the observer–the researcher, student or whoever–is drawing to visualize the items of knowledge and their relations, which have relevance for managers in certain situations. These pictures may concern individual managers or represent the view of a group of managers in general (for an example see Calori & Lawrence, 1991: 187). Such a picture or model of a real phenomenon must necessarily contain less than the real cognitive map, because a complete picture is not possible–the complexity of reality must be reduced in a picture or a model. The methods of recording and interpreting the underlying data and relations vary widely up to now. One critical point is here that most of these descriptions of knowledge items and their relations are given in a two-dimensional picture, which is quite insufficient to represent the complexity and dynamics of the underlying process. There are ways and possibilities to produce more complex and more realistic pictures either by using computer-aided dynamic models like the GAMMA-tool (Hub, 1994) or by adaptation of the Helidem-concept (Kahle & Wilms, 1998).

When the processes and structures of knowledge emergence and distribution such depicted are no individual traits but organizational ones, which means that they describe the existence and distribution of knowledge within and between groups (of managers), we have the third concept of cognitive maps, which is for enhancement of the difference attributed "organizational cognitive maps." They contain the systems of concepts and relations produced (Laukkanen, 1996: 28) or used (Taylor & Lerner, 1996: 260) by managers to understand their world and the strategies to cope with it. When these shared concepts of a group are visualized by an observer–mostly by diagrams of items and relations–we have the fourth of the levels of conceptualization of cognitive maps (for an example see Laukkanen, 1996: 10 ff.). In the following context, we refer mostly to the third and fourth level.

## *Implications of the Concept of Cognitive Maps for Organizational Theory*

The most important consequence of the introduction of this concept into organizational theory is the change of view concerning communication in organizations. Whereas up to this point it was accepted that organizations exist and develop by communication, it is now to be seen that organizations exist in communication (Taylor & Lerner, 1996: 260). It is quite acceptable to believe that managers discuss organizational topics and, in these discussions, find the rules and structures of organizations that make sense and utilize them. They interpret and modify those rules and structures, and produce organizational changes of the unplanned type in the continuous process (Staehle, 1994: 849).

The new view of organizational communication enhances this position and proceeds towards a concept in which the communication of managers is the organization. In this view communication includes the unsaid, but obvious, which is the most important aspect. Those items and relations which are so obvious that nobody mentions them but everybody is taking them for granted as necessary. Underlying assumptions of own decisions and actions are the core assumptions and values of an organization. These basic values and assumptions have been addressed as the basis of organizational culture (Schein, 1997: 16). The shared values and views of a group (of managers) need not be expressed explicitly, because they are known, believed and used by everybody. They are only discussed if and when there are differences about the implications of a value or a rule in a specific situation. The values and norms mostly are numerous and make a complex system. The explanations of the rules and values caused by such a doubt about implications and consequences of certain rules and values modify and re-interpret the rules and values, sometimes even the basic assumptions. There is normally no doubt in the validity of the values and rules, but a possible difference about the point, which rule or value is concerned in a certain situation and how conflicting prescriptions of different rules are solved. In a firm which is part of the tourism industry the managers will have an organizational cognitive map of the industry and their field of action, but with the increasing amount of new and partially contradictive information there will be much discussion about the interpretation of these information and the ways of action.

This concept of processes and structures of knowledge about organization which emerge by speaking about them and implying some shared assumptions and values, which in themselves make sense to the organizational actions of the managers, is in some way similar to the concept of organizational learning and the role of modeling within it (Morecroft & Sterman, 1994: XV and 6). In this concept of modeling, the development and use of models is not intended to provide the managers with tools for complicated optimization algorithms, which they do not really understand, but to create for them a model of the real world, a simplified picture of future developments, which they can grasp and understand through the modeling and in which they can try and train useful methods of analysis and ways of action. The models themselves are in this view not seen as instruments of analysis or optimization, but as arenas of discourse or as training areas.

This view on modeling is here widened and applied to managerial communication. So whenever managers speak about their joint actions and all that these actions involve, as for example the situation, the future developments including the invention of new products or techniques, the existing and possible competitors, the qualities and quantities of their own human resources and so on, they describe their individual cognitive maps (type 1) to the other managers. By discussion and by explicit or implicit acceptance they reach a shared cognitive map (type 3), which defines the stage at which each of them is acting their role. In military education very often the "sand table" is used as a tool for tactical practice. In this sand table a piece of landscape is built in a miniature form and an offensive or defensive situation is constructed. This sand table is now the cognitive map (type 4) for the group, which discusses and learns tactical and strategic actions.

For this group, the model–the landscape represented on the table– will become reality, so far as development and evaluation of tactical or strategic moves are concerned. The actors plan and conduct their actions and the quality of their planning is judged along orthodox tactics and strategies applicable in this model situation. Through this method the espoused theories of the group are not only shown in detail but they are continuously evaluated and modified. Afterwards, which means after having played numbers of such "war games," everybody knows the espoused tactics and strategies of his group and the managers will have the confidence that the other members of the group will understand their actions without much communication and they will accept the decisions, when they go along with the espoused theories, irrespective of the outcome of the actions. The information asymmetry between higher management or levels of command and the acting manager does not become more transparent, but easier to understand. In the tourism industry, where the planning process and the strategies are oriented at "campaigns" mostly consisting of a type of destination and a clearly defined timetable, the evaluation of the last campaign and the comparison with former campaigns is a widely used instrument and has the same results as the playing of "war-games."

## *Further Aspects of Cognitive Mapping in the Tourism Industry*

Beyond these basic implications of cognitive mapping for organizations there are three other aspects that should be considered. First, within the service rendering firms–the travel agencies, the carriers, the hotels–there are a great number of varying cognitive maps of type 3, which help to create the necessary variety (Ashby, 1958) to cope with complexity. This happens, because the individual cognitive maps (type 1) are not erased with the emergence of the type 3 maps, but stay along with the individual. The different groups in the organization, consisting of varying members, will create or allow different cognitive maps to emerge. The employees of the agencies, carriers or hotels have different experiences and often different cultural backgrounds. This induces diversity of the cognitive maps. Diversity and doubt lead to more flexibility of the strategic options of the tourism firms, but they threaten the stability of the organizational cognitive maps, which is needed for a clear understanding of each other. The organizational cognitive map is only a general way of speaking but no real phenomenon. It is the fictitious fuzzy quantity of shared assumptions and views.

The second and most important aspect of sense-making in the managerial communication is the making similar of the respective views, that is the adaptation of the individual views to the common view. Such a trivialization (von Foerster & Schmidt, 1996) is necessary for organizational processes of learning and for the diffusion of organizational innovations, because a unified and definite interpretation is necessary. This creates a contradiction to the point above, because flexibility requires a certain amount of diversity, whereas organizational acceptance needs clear-cut interpretations. With increasing numbers of participants in an organization, the stability will increase and the possibility for flexibility will decrease. For the firms in the tourism industry it is important to develop an accepted and understandable concept of the firms' activities and additionally for the employees and clients.

A third point is that new information in these cognitive maps is always connected selectively with the existing knowledge in such a way that the implications of the existing knowledge are maximized. This has to be examined very cautiously because misinterpretations may result. So if some very innovating information is introduced, which cannot be connected with the existing levels of information, it will not be considered any further due to the fact that it cannot be conceptualized against pre-learned experience or meaning.

A further consequence of these interpretations of organizational communications is a possible explication for the emergence or existence of strategic narrow sightedness or the groupthink syndrome (Radetzki, 1999: 68 f.). By the joint construction of their reality managers tend to exclude all information that does not stabilize this shared view. To create the model world or the sand table, problems have to be simplified, observations have to be unified and doubts are excluded. To solve a problem jointly, one needs a joint problem view. This is in most cases the simplest form of the problem, the minimum common denominator. When this is the accepted view in the group, other views and concepts for solving the problem are no longer accessible. The explicit use of cognitive map type 4 may help to clarify this dilemma of problem solving, because a meta-level of understanding is created (Kahle, 1995).

These general observations on cognitive maps can be applied to the tourism industry. We have the situation that in the five different stages or areas of the industry there exist various different forms of organizational arrangements and of knowledge transfer processes. The participants are culturally quite diverse (Bouncken, 2000: 91), so it can be expected that the cognitive maps of individuals and organizations from different countries will vary widely. By this greater variety the process of knowledge transfer will be impeded, because the implications of the information are less clear. On the other side this variety reduces the tendency towards group thinking, because the groups are confronted with an increase of contradicting information.

This problem of connectivity of one's own cognitive map with those of others in a field of many unknown and potentially different partners enhance the use of tried partners. With these tried partners one shares the experience of joint activities and a common understanding of situations and rules. This explains the possibility and the necessity of trust in these interorganizational and intercultural relations in the tourism industry (Bouncken, 2000: 92, 97).

## ASYMMETRIC INFORMATION
## IN THE PROCESSES OF TOURISM

### Forms of Asymmetric Information

Asymmetric information implies information deficits on one side of a transaction. This deficit may exist randomly or systematically in certain situations. The partners of a transaction are usually called "principal" and "agent," where the principal gets a certain result and the agent delivers (and produces) it. The five different parts of the tourism industry constitute together with the travelers a six-stage or six-level principal-agent problem. In effect each component within the system can be principal or agent depending upon the context of the situation concerned.

The basic assumptions, problems and possible solutions of principal-agent problems have been discussed widely (Picot, Dietl & Franck, 1999: 85-131; Jensen & Meckling, 1976; Pratt & Zeckhauser, 1985; Spremann, 1988, 1989, 1990), so we will, after a brief description of the core problems, focus on the industry-specific aspects.

There are four kinds of asymmetries related to the different attributes of the situation between the principal and the agent: "Hidden Characteristics," "Hidden Actions," "Hidden Information" and "Hidden Intentions." They are connected with each other and there are a number of possible actions to deal with these asymmetries, which shall be discussed under the specific aspect of tourism industry.

Hidden characteristics imply that the agents or their products have attributes known to themselves, but not made known to the principals. Akerlof (1970) first discussed this problem for the market of used cars, where the seller knows what is wrong (or not) with his car. The potential buyers aren't aware of the "real" condition of the vehicle and are therefore only willing to pay the price for an "average" car. Therefore the good cars will not be offered in the market which means that cars in average condition will be of an increasingly lower standard. This "adverse selection" leads to "a market of lemons." In the tourism industry, the carriers are possibly in a comparable situation in respect to their quality and security standards and their price policy: The travelers cannot know or evaluate (this would be a case of hidden information) the good or bad standards of the various carriers, so they are only willing to pay the average standard; therefore better standards will vanish from the market and the average will deteriorate.

Hidden action is possible, if the agents deliver their product or service that can be evaluated by the principals but those cannot see how the agents have carried out the work. So the agents may make less effort than they have promised and the principals can do nothing to further the efforts. This is typical for the "back office" operations in the tourism industry which are unseen and may cost much less than the fees that the travelers have to pay. If the travelers ask for a special or personal (tailor-made) travel product, it can be easily produced since the agency has accumulated so much information about the products. But the travelers are charged them more than the standard fees. For the tour operators the problem of hidden action lies with the carriers and hotels, whose performance is not directly observable. There are instruments such as monitoring to make observations, and sometimes the open observation of an employee by the principal is helpful, although it induces second order agency problems.

Hidden information is much similar to hidden action, only that here the principals may be able to observe the agents and their efforts, but they have no means to evaluate the efforts. That is typically so with knowledge based operations, where the principals cannot evaluate the quality of the knowledge of the agents (that could be a hidden characteristic) and the effort of the knowledge retrieval and use. The risk lying in all both these kinds of asymmetric information is the "moral hazard," the opportunity for the agent to "cheat."

In the case of hidden intentions it is assumed that there are conflicting goals (at least partially) between principals and agents, and the agents do not state that fact before the agreement. At a later stage the agents can–within the limits of the contract–further their own goals at the disadvantage of the principals. In the tourism industry this may happen, for example, when the traveler is at the destination and services, and have to pay extra although the tour package is inclusive. This is called a "Hold Up" situation (Goldberg, 1980).

### *Forms of Reduction the Risks of Asymmetric Information*

There is a great number of possible actions to reduce the moral hazard, either on the agent or principal side (Picot, Dietl & Franck, 1999: 91; Dixit & Nalebuff, 1993: 95; Kahle, 2002b: 26). Some of the actions can be used on either side. Actions for the principal are screening and monitoring. Actions for the agent only are signaling, guarantees, securities, building up reputation and destroying bridges to opportunistic behavior. Whereas contracts, developing trust by teamwork, ceasing communication, automatic responses, small steps and using "professional" intermediates are possible instruments for either side.

The use of these activities to reduce the risks of asymmetric information is expensive which the travelers normally will not be willing to pay. To achieve a maximum of efficiency the costs of risk reduction should be minimized. Monitoring activities to reduce risks that are known to the agents are the most important. The next important instrument is building up reputation as a quality brand. Then follows in importance guarantees to the travelers as a token of commitment. The division of activities between principals and agents depends mostly on the market position. Who gains more from the process will take the risk reduction measure.

The least-cost-activity–in monetary terms–to reduce the risk is trust as a reciprocal relation. Trust needs no monitoring nor any other instruments and therefore does not cost money. Trust is a good "sui generis" (Schulze, 1997: 70) that losses and gains are counted in other than monetary dimensions. Therefore, trust is the important dimension in the tourism industry. The importance has grown with the increased amount of information and the increased velocity of information processing. Trust is the core criterion in defining a network with the least-cost to reduce the risk of asymmetric information.

## *CONCLUSION*

The tourism industry has all the necessary features to be characterized as a "new economy" industry. The abundance of available information, the high velocity of information transfer, the change of transaction cost structure and the impacts of the special attributes of knowledge assets in an intercultural area of action create a special situation for the people involved in the tourism industry. The advantages of the developing new economy will only be secured if they are matched with stable relations to known and trusted partners. An important instrument for the better understanding and functioning of trust between these partners is the concept of cognitive maps. The use of this concept gives a cognitive basis to the trusted relations and will enhance understanding between the involved partners. Such a cognition-based trust will be able to reduce the problems of asymmetric information in the relations within the tourism industry.

## REFERENCES

Akerlof, G.A. (1970). The Market for "Lemons": Quality Uncertainty and the Market Mechanism, Quarterly Journal of Economics, vol. 89, pp. 488-500.

Ashby, R.W. (1958). Requisite variety and its implication for the control of complex systems, Cybernetica, 1/1958, pp. 83ff.

Böhme, G. (1998). Trau, schau, wem? Die Zeit, 16th December 1998, p. 45.

Bouncken, R.B. (2000). The Effect of Trust on Quality in the Culturally Diverse Tourism Industry, Journal of Quality Assurance in Hospitality and Tourism, vol. 1 no. 3, pp. 85-104.

Bourgeois III, L.J., Eisenhardt, K.M. (1988). Strategic Decision Processes in High Velocity Environments: Four Cases in the Microcomputer Industry, Management Science, vol. 34, no. 7, pp. 816-835.

Calori, R. & Lawrence, P. (eds.) (1991). The Business of Europe-Managing Change, London-Newbury Park-New Delhi: Sage.

Corsten, H. (1985). Die Produktion von Dienstleistungen, Wiesbaden: Gabler.

Dixit, A.K., Nalebuff, B.J. (1993). Thinking Strategically–The Competitive Edge in Business, Politics, and Everyday Life, New York-London: Norton.

Fischer, S. (2001). Virtuelle Unternehmen im interkulturellen Austausch-Möglichkeiten und Grenzen von Kooperation in Netzwerken, Wiesbaden: Gabler-duv.

Gerum, E. (2001). Unternehmensnetzwerke: Ein Grundlagenstreit, Paper für den Workshop der Kommission Wissenschaftstheorie im Verband der Hochschullehrer für Betriebswirtschaft, Augsburg 29.30.6.2001 (forthcoming).

Goldberg, V.P. (1980). Relational Exchange. Economics and Complex Contracts, American Behavioral Scientist, vol. 23, pp. 337-352.

Hall, E.T., Reed Hall, M. (1990). Understanding Cultural Differences, Yarmouth: Intercultural Press.

Hecker, M. (1999). Informationsüberflutung und deren Vermeidung, Hamburg: Dr. Kovac.

Hofstede, G. (1982). Culture's Consequences, International Differences in Work-Related Values, abridged edition, Beverly Hills, CA: Sage.

Hofstede, G. (1993). Interkulturelle Zusammenarbeit: Kulturen-Organisationen-Management, Wiesbaden: Gabler.

Hub, H. (1994). Für Einsteiger und Trainer: Eine Methodik zum PC-Werkzeug GAMMA-an einem Beispiel demonstriert, Beitrag 2, Hub, H. (Hrsg.): Komplexe Aufgabenstellungen ganzheitlich bearbeiten–Fallstudien und Beispiele aus der Praxis, Deutsche Management Gesellschaft e.V., Nürtingen.

Jensen, M.C., Meckling, W.H. (1976) Theory of the Firm: Managerial Behavior, Agency Costs and Ownership Structure, Journal of Financial Economics, vol. 3, pp. 305-360.

Kahle, E. (1995). Remarks on the Cognitional Basis of Understanding, Self-understanding and Self-Organization, Arbeitsbericht 03/95 der Forschungsgruppe Kybernetische Unternehmensstrategie–FOKUS–Universität Lüneburg. Lüneburg.

Kahle, E., Wilms, F.E.P. (1998). Der Helidem–Eine nichthierarchische Form der Analyse komplexer Wirkungsgefüge, Aachen: Shaker.

Kahle, E. (2001). Betriebliche Entscheidungen, 6. Auflage, München-Wien: Oldenbourg.

Kahle, E. (2002a). Verändern sich ökonomische Gesetze in der New Economy oder nur ihre Anwendungsbedingungen, Bleicher, K., Berthel, J., Auf dem Weg in die Wissensgesellschaft, Frankfurt: FAZ Buch, pp. 175-189.

Kahle, E. (2002b). Security Management unter HR-und Organisationsaspekten, Personalführung 5/2002, pp. 22-31.

Kahle, E. (2002c). Virtuelle Organisationen unter besonderer Berücksichtigung kultureller Barrieren, Scholz, Ch. (ed.), Systemdenken und Virtualisierung-Unternehmensstrategien zur Vitalisierung und Virtualisierung auf der Grundlage von Systemtheorie und Kybernetik, Berlin: Duncker + Humblot, pp. 93-108.

Kelley, K. (1997). New Rules for the New Economy, San Francisco: Jossey-Bass.

Küsters, E. (1998), Episoden des interkulturellen Managements, Wiesbaden: Gabler-duv.

Langeard, E. (1981). Grundlagen des Dienstleistungsmarketings, Zeitschrift für Forschung und Praxis, vol. 3, no. 4, pp. 233-240.

Laukkanen, M. (1996). Comparative Cause Mapping of Organizational Cognitions. Meindl, J.R., Stubbart, Ch., Porac, J.F. (Ed.), Cognition Within and Between Organizations, Thousand Oaks et al.: Sage, pp. 3-44.

Luhmann, N. (1989). Vertrauen-Ein Mechanismus der Reduktion sozialer Komplexität, 3. Auflage, Stuttgart: Schäfer-Pöschel.

Morecroft, J.-D. W., Sterman., J. D. (Ed.). (1994). Modeling for Learning Organizations, Portland: Productivity Press.

Nonaka, I., Boysiere, P., Borucki, C.C. et al. (1994). Organizational Knowledge Creation Theory: A First Comprehensive Test, International Business Review, vol. 3, no.4, pp. 337-351.

Piaget, J. (1979). Sprechen und Denken des Kindes, 4. Auflage, Düsseldorf: Pädagogischer Verlag Schwann.

Picot, A., Dietl, H., Franck, E. (1999). Organisation–Eine ökonomische Perspektive, 2. Auflage, Stuttgart: Schäfer-Pöschel.

Polanyi, M. (1966). The Tacit Dimension, Garden City, NY: Doubleday.

Pratt, J.W., Zeckhauser, R.J. (1985). Principals and Agents: The Structure of Business, Boston: Harvard Business School Press.

Radetzki, Th. (1999). Multipersonelles Verhalten bei strategischen Entscheidungen, Wiesbaden: Gabler-duv.

Rode, N. (2001). Wissensmarketing–Strategische Entscheidungsoptionen für Wissensanbieter, Wiesbaden: Gabler.

Schein, E.H. (1997). Organizational Culture and Leadership (2 ed.), San Francisco: Jossey-Bass.

Schulze, M. (1997). Profit in der Non-Profit-Organisation–Ein betriebswirtschaftlicher Ansatz zur Klärung der Definitionsdiskussion, Wiesbaden: Gabler-duv.

Spremann, K. (1988). Reputation, Garantie, Information, Zeitschrift für Betriebswirtschaft, vol. 58, pp. 613-629.

Spremann, K. (1989). Agent and Principal, Bamberg, G., Spremann, K. (Hrsg.): Agency Theory, Information and Incentives, Berlin et al.: Springer, pp. 3-37.

Spremann, K. (1990). Asymmetrische Information, Zeitschrift für Betriebswirtschaft, vol. 60, pp. 561-586.

Staehle, W.H. (1994). Management. Eine verhaltensorientierte Perspektive. 7. Ed., München: Vahlen.

Taylor, J., Lerner, L. (1996). Making Sense of Sensemaking: How Managers Construct Their Organization Through Their Talk, Studies in Cultures, Organizations and Societies, vol. 2, no. 2, pp. 257-286.

Theisen, P. (1970). Grundzüge einer Theorie der Beschaffungspolitik, Berlin: Duncker + Humblot.

von Foerster, H., Schmidt, S.J. (1996). Wissen und Gewissen: Versuch einer Brücke. Frankfurt: Suhrkamp.

Williamson, O.E. (1985). The Incentive Limits of Firms: A Comparative Institutional Assessment of Bureaucracy, Weltwirtschaftliches Archiv, pp. 736-763.

# Knowledge Management
# for Quality Improvements in Hotels

Ricarda B. Bouncken

**SUMMARY.** Hotels can improve their service quality by enhancing employees' knowledge about customer's preferences and the corresponding service procedures. Service quality depends strongly on the ability of hotels to acquire, to develop, to accumulate, and to distribute knowledge assets. Despite the popularity of knowledge management in other industries, hotel-specific concerns have been largely neglected in the literature and knowledge management has just rudimentarily been implemented in hotels. Especially hotel chains, which have to deliver an overall quality standard in geographically distributed hotels, can exploit knowledge management's benefits. Nevertheless, the implementation of knowledge management requires considerations. This article describes knowledge management in hotels, presents case-studies and gives strategic advice and structural recommendations for its implementation. An examination of hotels' knowledge management requires theoretical underpinning. Therefore, this article provides reflections about knowledge and analyzes different dimensions of knowledge management in hotels. Further, it presents major influences on

Ricarda B. Bouncken is Chair for Planning and Innovation Management, Brandenburg University of Technology Cottbus, Erich-Weinert-Str. 1 03044 Cottbus, Germany (E-mail: bouncken@tu-cottbus.de).
The author would like to express gratitude to Accor Hotels (Mr. Cisco, Human Resources; Mr. Senger, Human Resource Director; Mrs. Werner, Assistant General Management), to Best Western Hotels (Mr. Smola, Manager Hotel Services), and to Maritim Hotels (Mrs. Lindemann, Marketing Manager) for the interviews.

[Haworth co-indexing entry note]: "Knowledge Management for Quality Improvements in Hotels." Bouncken, Ricarda B. Co-published simultaneously in *Journal of Quality Assurance in Hospitality & Tourism* (The Haworth Hospitality Press, an imprint of The Haworth Press, Inc.) Vol. 3, No. 3/4, 2002, pp. 25-59; and: *Knowledge Management in Hospitality and Tourism* (ed: Ricarda B. Bouncken and Sungsoo Pyo) The Haworth Hospitality Press, an imprint of The Haworth Press, Inc., 2002, pp. 25-59. Single or multiple copies of this article are available for a fee from The Haworth Document Delivery Service [1-800-HAWORTH, 9:00 a.m. - 5:00 p.m. (EST). E-mail address: docdelivery@haworthpress.com].

10.1300/J162v03n03_03

strategic and structural aspects of knowledge management in hotels and suggests structures for the implementation of a knowledge management. *[Article copies available for a fee from The Haworth Document Delivery Service: 1-800-HAWORTH. E-mail address: <docdelivery@haworthpress.com> Website: <http://www.HaworthPress.com> © 2002 by The Haworth Press, Inc. All rights reserved.]*

**KEYWORDS.** Hotels, knowledge management, interfirm communication, service quality

## INTRODUCTION

The major task of hotels is to promote customer satisfaction and loyalty while establishing a competitive advantage (Nightingale, 1985). A major factor on customer satisfaction and loyalty is quality (Fallon & Schofield, 2000: 30). Hotel guest's quality perception is mainly influenced by the service encounter that can range between seconds and months and is determined by the type of hotels, and the type of hotel guests with different service experiences (Medlik, 1990: 10f.; Teare, Mazanec, Crawford-Welch, & Calver, 1994: 6; Powers, 1995: 19). Therefore, hotels require staff which are able to cope with different guests and their preferences. However, many quality problems occur because the staff does not fully understand the consequences of service interactions and guest's preferences. Consequently, improving employees' knowledge about customer's preferences and the corresponding service procedures is becoming increasingly important in hotels. This requires the retrieval and utilization of other staff members' experiences that suffers from:

- a high rate of employee turnover (bearing risk of knowledge loss),
- a high rate rotating employees between hotels (forcing to build up new team knowledge),
- a high percentage of unskilled workers or a low status employees (Keiser, 1989: 113f.) (necessity to build up standards, knowledge and foster learning), and
- irregular and seasonal demand and changing customer preferences confronting a stable capacity (problems of volatility and flexibility) (Keiser, 1989: 122).

Consequently, hotels have to save experiences, which should not be lost, when employees leave the hotel or rotate between hotels. They also need to support unskilled workers and new employees with other employees' experiences, build up easily understandable standards and foster learning. Hotels can particularly benefit from a knowledge management system, which helps to transfer and save knowledge within the hotel and supports the staff's service interactions. Hence, knowledge management, which has recently emerged as a means of improving business performance (Spender, 1994; Grant, 1996; Teece, 1984), needs to be implemented and improved regarding the specific requirements in hotels. Knowledge management must help to identify, generate, accumulate, save, retrieve, and distribute knowledge to contribute towards improving company-wide service quality. Nevertheless, knowledge management in hotels can benefit from the service encounter that offers the possibility to achieve knowledge directly about existing and changing customer expectations.

Despite the popularity of knowledge management in other industries, hotel-specific concerns have thus been neglected in the literature and knowledge management has just rudimentarily been implemented in hotels. This is especially valid for hotel chains, which have to deliver an overall quality standard in geographically distributed hotels (Medlik, 1990: 153).

To fill the identified gap the paper concentrates on hotel chains. First, the paper analyzes the theoretical background of knowledge, which affects a knowledge management strongly in hotels. Here, matters of discussion are diverse forms of knowledge that require specific ways of knowledge retrieval, transfer and accumulation. Second, strategy and structure based recommendations on knowledge management in hotels will be explained. This article provides a reflection on forms and criteria that determine the knowledge strategy in hotels. It also supplies the reader with insights about different instruments, which facilitate the identification, generation, accumulation, and distribution of knowledge. A major impact on hotels' knowledge management has a hybrid knowledge based strategy of personalization and codification (see Figure 1). According to the envisaged form of knowledge a personal transfer, retrieval, and conservation or a codified transfer, retrieval, and conservation is suitable.

## THEORETICAL BACKGROUND
## OF KNOWLEDGE MANAGEMENT

Scientists, managers, and consultants provide us with different perspectives of knowledge and an unequivocal definition of knowledge (Senge, 1990; Nonaka, 1991; von Krogh, Roos, & Slocum, 1994;

FIGURE 1. Elements of Knowledge Management

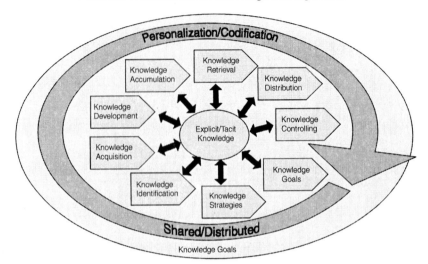

Grant, 1996; Drucker, Dyson, Handy, Saffo, & Senge, 1997; Drucker, 1999; Lathi, 2000). This paper follows the cognitive and constructivist understanding of knowledge (Spencer Brown, 1969; von Foerster, 1984; Luhmann, 1985; von Glasersfeld, 1997), which concentrates on social processes of knowledge generation and understands knowledge as interpreted and interconnected information (von Foerster, 1998: 44; von Glasersfeld, 1998: 19; Luhmann, 2000: 100-102; Mir & Watson, 2000: 943).

While different forms of knowledge are notable, and these have different implications on knowledge transfer and utilization, we need to select and to distinguish between major forms of knowledge. A popular differentiation exists since Polanyi distinguished explicit and tacit knowledge (Polanyi, 1967). Explicit knowledge is open to codification in documents, books, databases, and reports (Lathi, 2000: 66). Formal processes like a methodical language offer mechanisms to transfer explicit knowledge. Instead, tacit knowledge is very complex, involves viewpoints, intuition, deeply grounded statements, meaningful behavior, and values that people develop through experience (Nonaka, Byosiere, Borucki, & Konno, 1994; Leonard & Sensiper, 1998: 113). The transfer of tacit knowledge requires a process of understanding that is near to action, commitment, and involvement in a specific context (Nonaka & Tageuchi,

1995). Tacit knowledge contains cognitive and "technical" elements. Cognitive elements like paradigms, schemes, and beliefs help individuals to understand the environment. Technical elements enclose skills and embedded know-how for specific actions.

The transfer of knowledge always requires finding redundancy and connections between the items of the individual mind and the transferred knowledge. Therefore, direct interrelations that are richer with information foster the transfer of identical or tacit knowledge (see: Chapter 5.1).

A second major categorization of knowledge differentiates individual and collective knowledge, which contains commonly held knowledge. Individual knowledge can be perceived as sources individuals use for their actions and cognitions (Boisot, 1998: 12). There is a great similarity between individual knowledge and individual mental models from a cognitive point of view. The literature understands mental models as internal symbolic representations of the world or aspects of the world (Johnson-Laird, 1983). An individual's mental model concerning a specific topic includes the individual's definitions, procedures, examples, etc. (Carley, 1997: 535). Mental models employ tacit and implicit knowledge.

The literature often focuses on individual knowledge in organizations, but a great amount of knowledge is produced and held collectively in firms (Seely Brown & Duguid, 1998: 91). Organizational knowledge originally founded in collectively held models compromises know-what and know-how, which several organization members share. While the firms' competencies to outperform the marketplace lie in the ongoing generation and synthesis of collective, organizational knowledge, for firms to add value from knowledge it is especially relevant to build up organizational knowledge (Leonard, 1995; Seely Brown & Duguid, 1998). Nonaka thus concentrates on organizational knowledge creation, which he understands as the "capability of a company as a whole to create new knowledge, disseminate it throughout the organization, and embody it in products, services, and systems" (Nonaka & Tageuchi, 1995: 3).

The organizational knowledge literature focuses either on shared knowledge in the organization or on distributed knowledge that exists with reference of the organization (Kim, 1993: 41ff.; Lyles, 1994: 460). In the case of shared knowledge, only redundant mental models act as organizational models. This neglects the positive effects of combined specialized knowledge bases in firms. Therefore, organizational knowledge should contain shared knowledge (mental models) and distributed knowledge (mental model), which are pooled with reference of the organization.

## CATEGORIES OF KNOWLEDGE IN HOTELS

Offering services in lodging, food, recreation, and sports hotels have complex work processes and guest interfaces that can be differentiated in categories of knowledge:

- task-specific knowledge,
- task-related knowledge,
- transactive memory, and
- guest-related knowledge.

*Task-specific knowledge* contains the specific procedures, sequences, actions and strategies to fulfill a task (Cannon-Bowers & Salas, 2001: 196f.). Task-specific knowledge is only open to generalization of a similar task's other instances (Cannon-Bowers & Salas, 2001: 197). Task-specific knowledge allows employees to act in a coordinated way, without the need to communicate extensively (Cannon-Bowers, Salas, & Converse, 1993). Explicit and tacit components of task-specific knowledge secure goal fulfillment in firms. Common task-specific knowledge in hotels fosters compatible expectations of tasks and outcomes. Often details of task-specific knowledge can be articulated and codified, but need to be internalized by training. Task-specific knowledge contains, e.g., specified front- and back-office operations, which can be codified in documents or databases, but need to be trained and made into a routine aspect for the enhancement of service quality in hotels. Task-specific know-how contains a high rate of tacit knowledge and internalized service routines in hotels, which allow continuous service quality in hotels. The transfer of task-specific know-how required training, advisory, and exercise. Internalized and trained task-specific knowledge allows service procedures with less cognitive attention and reflection to the specific task. This enhances employees' mental capacity to listen to the guest, fulfill specific preferences, act friendly, and develop new or alternative service operations. The guests' service quality perception can be improved.

*Task-related knowledge* contains individuals' shared knowledge not of a single task, but of related tasks, e.g., the form of teamwork in the firm (Rentsch, Heffner, & Duffy, 1994). Task-related knowledge contributes to the team's or group's ability to internalize similar working values or to fulfill a broader task and intertwined tasks. Task-related knowledge contributes to the shared values of teamwork, but also compromises the ability to reach a distinct level of quality in different service operations. Shared quality standards in the different departments (lodging, food and recreation) where different tasks have to be fulfilled act as common task-related knowledge. Quality dimensions like empathy, reliability, and assurance in different service operations are examples for task-related knowledge. Although task-related can be articulated, service personnel need to internalize the task-related quality standards and behavioral rules. The broadest category of task-related knowledge are shared values, norms and beliefs, e.g., shared beliefs (Cannon & Edmondson, 2001) and cognitive consensus in the organization (Mohammed, Klimoski, & Rentsch, 2000). Shared attitudes and beliefs foster compatible interpretations of the environment. Further common attitudes, norms and beliefs support a mutual understanding of interrelating employees. Shared values, norms, and beliefs that lead the behavior and attitudes of employees can also guide task-specific knowledge and the quality of service operations.

At Hyatt, they believe that a great hotel should offer more than a good night's sleep. It should create an environment that awakens guests' senses. This is one of the many intangible qualities a guest should experience at every Hyatt hotel. These statements illustrate values at Hyatt, which are task-related knowledge. Maritim hotels follow five cornerstones of cosmopolitan attitude, hospitality, individuality, open-mindedness, and professional congress and special-event facilities. Ritz Carlton hotels strive for indulgent luxury with sumptuous surroundings and legendary service and gracious elegance. Shared values and norms act as groundbreaking levels of customer service. Ritz Carlton employees shared values collectively called The Gold Standards: The Credo, The Three Steps of Service, The Motto and The Twenty Basics. All 22,000 employees of The Ritz-Carlton know, embrace and energize this task-related knowledge, aided by their constant presence in the written form of a pocket-sized, laminated card. The Gold Standards are introduced for new employees' orientation. Thereafter, the concepts are reinforced in daily departmental "line-ups" attended by all employees. The Gold Standards provide the basis for all ongoing employee training.

A *transactive memory* includes decentralized knowledge of the other organizational members' cognitive models ([Wegner, 1985 #1740; Wegner, 1987; Wegner, 1995 #1681]). Transactive memory's relevance lies in the circumstance that working partners need to understand some of the others' knowledge, preferences, weaknesses, and work values. However, a transactive memory does not presume a high level of sharing; it consists of intertwined distributed mental models. The shared elements are concerning the common interrelations and connections between the members. A transactive memory corresponds to know-who, to find the right person for a specific task. The time and intensity of interacting members promotes the generation of a transactive memory system. A transactive memory assists goal fulfillment by helping members to compensate for each other, predict each other's action, provide information before being asked, and support the connection of the members' expert knowledge (Cannon-Bowers & Salas, 2001: 197). While working together for a longer period, members are better able to predict the others' behavior in accordance with what they expect from them. Hence, each member of the transactive memory has a better understanding of the others' idiosyncratic knowledge and competencies. Knowledge in the concept of transactive memory can be task-specific, task-related, or useful across a variety of tasks. Hence, a transactive memory system contains team-specific knowledge. A transactive memory can be found in all team structures and in hotels (e.g., in front and back-office teams). Moreover, a transactive memory exists when employees know about other colleagues' knowledge in the hotel chain. Various connections may occur in regional dispersed hotels (e.g., between hotel directors in different regions or countries).

### Guest-Related Knowledge

While staff and guest interrelate directly in the service encounter guests' expectations and actions influence many operations in hotels. Customers' requests have impacts on one or more employees, and can modify task-specific or task-related knowledge in a hotel or more hotels and can require inter-hotel learning. Therefore, customer interactions are tangled with task-specific knowledge, task-related knowledge, transactive memory, and shared attitudes, norms, values and beliefs. Customer-related knowledge includes the knowledge of:

- What a specific customer actually wants,
- what a specific customer of the hotel chain wishes in the future, and
- what customers in a hotel's target group generally desire.

Cohen and Levinthal label the firm's ability to recognize the value of new, external knowledge, to assimilate it and apply it to its new products and services as absorptive capacity (Cohen & Levinthal, 1990: 128; Van den Bosch, Volberda, & de Boer, 1999). As hotels have direct customer interactions, absorptive capacity concentrates on customer relationship and the acquisition of customer related knowledge. For example, a customer may initiate new meal patterns or recommend new services. Absorptive capability depends on the firm's level of prior related knowledge because prior accumulated knowledge enhances the acquisition of new knowledge and the ability to remember and use knowledge (Cohen & Levinthal, 1990; Lane & Lubatkin, 1998: 464f.). The premise of the dependence on prior knowledge stresses the importance of the personal service experience for knowledge generation. Associative learning develops the ability to generate new knowledge, which requires establishing links between different stocks of knowledge and connections between old and new knowledge. Consequently, individual and organizational knowledge limits the ability to absorb customer related knowledge and to exploit new opportunities (Leonard, 1995: 189-200). Additionally, a hotel's absorptive capacity refers not only to the individual's capacity but also to the hotel's competence in accumulating and exploiting knowledge. This stresses the acquisition, transfer, and accumulation of customer-related knowledge between staff and hotel and the transfer of knowledge between the subunits of a hotel chain.

## KNOWLEDGE MANAGEMENT SYSTEM IN HOTELS

### Overview

Knowledge management facilitates a continuous progress in learning and unlearning to ensure the renewal of organizational goals, as well to promote organizational awareness to better anticipate opportunities and threats (Young & McCuiston, 2000: 315). Therefore, hotels can enhance their service quality. The implementation of knowledge management requires a systemic knowledge orientated adaptation of hard and soft factors in hotels. Soft factors generally include openness, trust, respect, frames of reference, values, beliefs, an orientation toward continuous development and expanded personal communication (Lyles, 1994: 461). Hard factors fostering the acquisition, retrieval and storing of internal and external knowledge can contain databases, libraries, communication technologies and seminars or organizational structures. Both factors influence service quality, while service includes "a package of implicit and explicit benefits performed within a supporting facility and using facilitating goods" (Fitzsimmons & Fitzsimmons, 1994: 24). Knowledge management requires the combination of different activities in hotels. Although knowledge management combines these tightly intertwined activities and implementation possibilities, tools and structures to foster the activities generally fulfill different purposes and are applicable to different knowledge processes. Nevertheless, to give an understanding of the knowledge management as a continuous management concept, the following explains the elements stepwise.

### Knowledge Goals

To determine the field and the directions of knowledge acquisition, generation, distribution, retrieval and accumulation, hotels can set specific goals concerning inter-hotel and intra-hotel knowledge management (e.g., an Internet-based information system might be installed). Knowledge goals can also be formulated to enhance the acquisition and utilization of customer-related knowledge. Therefore, guest cards, which contain all data of frequent clients can be implemented enabling front- and back-office to organize guests preferences immediately after booking. Moreover, guests' satisfaction will be improved when the guest receives automatically her preferred rooms or services. Knowledge goals might also concentrate on better communication with tourist offices to give the possibility of absorbing regional trends more easily.

Best Western International, Inc., is the world's largest hotel brand with more than 4,000 independently owned and operated hotels throughout Australia, Asia and Southern Africa, Canada, the Caribbean, Europe, the Middle East, Mexico, Central and South America and the United States. It is also the only non-profit membership association in the industry. Although Best Western accomplishes a franchise system with limited hierarchical power to the hotels, they explicitly follow the vision that all hotels should exploit every chance transferring or utilizing their employees' knowledge. Best Western assumes that knowledge is the basis for superior service quality leading to competitive advantage. Since Best Western aims to improve their hotels' knowledge base they provide a range of infrastructure and programs to their franchise partners. A training institute offers seminars at a reduced rate for their partners. Besides, international and regional conferences explain Best Western's corporate strategy and allow informal knowledge transfer between ho-

tel management. Best Western installed an intranet to provide infrastructure for the hotels' knowledge transfer. Employees are able to
retrieve, accumulate and distribute specific topics in the Internet-based
intranet. Best Western strives for enhanced generation and employment
of organizational knowledge in the future.

### Knowledge Strategy

On the foundation of knowledge goals, hotels can establish different
knowledge-oriented strategies influencing many elements on a knowledge management system. Often knowledge strategies concentrate on
enhanced knowledge transfer between different stakeholders. Knowledge transfer contains the exchange and utilization of knowledge within
the firm, with other firms, and with the customer. It happens in the hotel
between:

- staff in the hotel,
- customer and staff in hotels,
- top-management in the hotel and staff,
- top-management of the different hotels in a hotel chain,
- regional tourist offices/government and hotel staff, and
- regional destination management/government and hotel's top management.

Moreover, knowledge strategies often determine the degree of sharing
of employees' mental models (see Chapter 5.1 (Shared or Distributed
Knowledge in Hotels?)). Shared models allow better understanding, but
hinder specialization. Consequently, two dimensions of knowledge-
based strategies exist:

- the degree of shared mental models (shared knowledge vs. distributed knowledge) and
- the form of knowledge transfer (codification vs. personalization).

Firms can transfer explicit knowledge easily through media as books, databases, or libraries organization wide (see Chapter 5.2 (Personalized or Codified Knowledge Transfer?)). On the contrary, the transfer of implicit
knowledge requires personnel interaction and understanding. The codification strategy supports the codification of knowledge by extracting it from
the person who generated the knowledge, and storing it into databases
(Hansen, Nohria, & Tierney, 1999). Thereby, firms extract knowledge

from persons and achieve person-independent knowledge that everyone in the firm can retrieve. Personalization strategy focuses on people as knowledge sources. Thus, an improved retrieval of internal experts and social operations strengthens knowledge management. A codification strategy with a technology-centered viewpoint often disheartens people-centered activities (Marchant, Kettinger, & Rollins, 2000: 69). Hotels striving for improved behavioral patterns, norms and values should concentrate on personalization.

### Knowledge Identification

The formulation and foundation of knowledge goals requires an identification of strategic knowledge requirements. These include evaluation criteria, the determination of the knowledge gap, and the specific narrowing of the knowledge gap (Post, 1999: 137). Hotels like other firms have insufficient knowledge about their internal knowledge. Because of a large number of employees and geographically dispersed hotels, hotels lose overview about their distributed knowledge base. In order to draw up a specific knowledge strategy, the first step is often a survey of existing knowledge (Schreinemakers, 1999) and the determination of required knowledge, which entails the identification of relevant knowledge. Hotels have to consider the relevance of specific knowledge in order to prevent a simple accumulation of irrelevant knowledge, which nobody in the hotel can deploy. Different techniques have been established in the literature and in companies to identify knowledge in firms. Hotels with their high amount of working routines and rotating employees in dispersed hotels have difficulties in identifying their high ratio of embedded tacit knowledge. The identification of all knowledge is impossible due to the dynamic character of knowledge and the embeddedness of know-how and tacit knowledge. However, interviewing employees, analyzing customer databases, starting knowledge circles, and organizing meetings between different employees improves knowledge's identification in hotels. More than in other industries hotels can benefit from observation of service operations. In those service operations tacit knowledge becomes apparent and observable.

### Knowledge Acquisition and Development

Knowledge acquisition and development follow different foci, but are closely related because they improve knowledge generation. Knowledge acquisition concentrates on external knowledge retrieval from customers, external experts, tourist office, etc., and often enhances the assimilation of previously unnoticed trends. Knowledge development focuses on the internal processes to increase knowledge (Lathi, 2000: 67) and enclose activities that span from creating new insights and concepts to the generation of new behavioral patterns and service operations. Knowledge develops via service research and development and via service practice in hotels. Research contains the exploration of databases and experimentation with new service procedures. Observed new consumer trends can guide new service operations as well. New operations or concepts may be tested in specific hotels. Successful operations will be implemented afterwards in different hotels. The internal development generally requires the distribution of knowledge and the cooperation of different employees in hotels. To come into action, firms need the ability to integrate the knowledge into practice and to distribute knowledge throughout the hotels. Therefore, knowledge management requires the establishment of mechanisms ensuring the learning and distribution of experiences and putting it into operations. For example, the generation of linkages between the new knowledge and the implementation in business operations or strategy can support putting knowledge into action.

Hotels can also acquire knowledge via external knowledge links. Knowledge links offer companies access to the skills and capabilities of other organizations that allows them to create new knowledge and capabilities (Badaracco, 1991: 107-128). Tourist offices and the region's government also act as important external sources of knowledge and knowledge links because of their knowledge of newer regional challenges and visitors' preferences. Especially direct personal interactions between hotel management and government/tourist office work as powerful knowledge links, which support the transfer of knowledge and facilitates shared knowledge between hotels and the tourist office encouraging successful integrative strategies of the destination.

## *Knowledge Accumulation, Retrieval, and Distribution*

While the large number of rotating staff and employee turnover limits the accumulation, retrieval and distribution of knowledge it is critical for hotels to foster staff loyalty and to protect organizational knowledge when employees leave the company.

Knowledge accumulation is concerned with the collection and the retrieval of knowledge in databases (codification) or from people (personalization). While staff have to use more than individually-held knowledge they must gain access to other people's private knowledge or to codified knowledge. Activities which facilitate knowledge's distribution are engaged to disperse knowledge in the hotel chain. Employees must have the ability to access knowledge company-wide that gives advisory and orientation for values, norms, specific projects, and service operations. Personal knowledge can be retrieved by networks of people who know the other's expertise (transactive memory) or by directly interrelating people. Codified knowledge can be found in databases and via search tools. Knowledge retrieval and the characteristics of the knowledge required have implications on the transfer of knowledge. The inter-hotel retrieval of knowledge is of great importance in hotel chains since lessons learned in one hotel, department, or team can be used to offer modified service operations, service extensions, and entire new service lines in other hotels. This allows quality improvements in hotels.

For the enhancement of a hotel's knowledge accumulation, retrieval, and distribution, it is essential to transfer knowledge between top-management (horizontal) and between top management and staff (vertical). Supporting internal knowledge transmission and distribution also helps accumulating and conserving knowledge in hotels because of redundant knowledge, which is held by the different employees in hotels.

### Knowledge Controlling

Hotels require the identification, development, and retrieval of relevant knowledge to establish an efficient knowledge management system. Implementing knowledge management hotels have also installed controlling devices that help to evaluate the fulfillment of knowledge goals. Knowledge controlling answers questions concerning:

- Is the knowledge-strategy still suitable?
- Does a changing environment imply adjustments?
- Did the hotel-chain or the specific hotel fulfill knowledge goals?
- How did they fulfill the goals?
- What department met the goals?
- To what degree were goals targeted?
- Which gaps still remain?
- What does identified gaps mean for new knowledge goals, strategies, and programs?

Controlling guides the adaptation of knowledge goals, strategies, and programs to enhance knowledge acquisition, development, accumulation, retrieval, and distribution is possible in single hotels or the entire hotel chain.

## KNOWLEDGE STRATEGY IN HOTELS

### Shared or Distributed Knowledge in Hotels?

Hotels installing knowledge management have to consider the advantages of shared or distributed mental models in the company. This questions:

- what the benefit of shared models is,
- what shall be shared, and
- how much sharing is necessary?

Different degrees of sharing are possible; the continuum ranges from exactly the same mental model to completely different mental models about a specific topic in the hotel chain. Due to a constructivist standpoint, individuals' complete sharing of all mental models is nearly impossible. Following an economic perspective, complete sharing contradicts specialization and is ineffective in firms. Nevertheless, shared (redundant) mental models enhance the transfer of knowledge and employees' understanding.

Although the literature does not provide information about an optimal level of shared mental models in general, we have to analyze more deeply the advantages and disadvantages of sharing in hotels. Shared respectively overlapping individual models allow improved coordination, communication, and result in superior performance, because they foster understanding and via redundancy the transfer of knowledge. Different empirical studies concerning sharing in teams show developed team processes, which result in superior team performance (Banks & Millward, 2000: 513; Heffner, Mathieu, & Cannon-Bowers, 1995; Heffner, Mathieu, & Goodwin, 1998). Stout et al. demonstrate that enlarged sharing across individual mental models permits better communication under a higher workload, which in turn offers a better coordinated team performance (Stout, Cannon-Bowers, Salas, & Milanovic, 1999). The underlying hypothesis for the benefit of shared mental models in organizations is that individual mental models build up matching and appropriate expectations and explanations of their work task and the company's goals.

Consequently, a high level of overlapping individual mental models guarantees employees' similar expectations of the task and team (Cannon-Bowers et al., 1993; Cannon-Bowers, Tannenbaum, Salas, & Volpe, 1995). Shared understanding supports the establishment of common explanations and expectations, which end in a better work coordination. This leads to improved goal fulfillment in hotels, in which the coordination of employees is of great importance for service quality.

Despite their positive effects, completely shared mental models in hotels resemble labor allowing all team members to do the same job and service operations. Inefficiency occurs, because the hotel cannot benefit from the specialization of its members. Service quality then suffers from the lack of synergies from expert knowledge and from reduced speed of team learning. Especially, if systems, tasks and actions are highly complex and variable, members must have accurate models about the task and the task fulfillment. This is especially valid for intense personal service operations in the service encounter. According to complex, varying or various service operations (e.g., business traveler, leisure traveler, recreation services, lodging services, food services, or events) in the complex environment, it is impossible for any single employee to hold all the required knowledge in hotels. Consequently, hotels require highly specialized knowledge and a distributed knowledge system. While nobody in the firm can oversee all knowledge if the firm exists as a distributed knowledge system (Tsoukas, 1996), the combination and connection of different distributed knowledge requires some shared issues as well. Therefore, linkages and redundancy between the mental models and of the employees involved in the same context (working together) are necessary in hotels.

Moreover, hotel chains comprise a number of different regionally dispersed hotels. These hotels intend to fulfill globally standardized quality standards, different customer needs, diverse tasks, and have to be able to cope with staff from different countries. The question whether to promote shared mental models or distributed models is also essential in hotel chains. Hotels need distributed and shared mental models. Distributed models are necessary because a high percentage of unskilled workers and employees with lower learning capacities need to fulfill the worldwide dispersed organization's tasks and quality standards. In the case of distributed organizational knowledge, employees do not have to learn the whole amount of knowledge in the system. This allows high quality services while attaining tasks more easily. Therefore, hotels have to establish especially distributed models in case of task-specific knowledge.

However, a high turnover of staff often has the implication of a high risk of knowledge drain. Therefore, hotels require shared models as well. A knowledge drain occurs when employees leave the company and take their individual task-specific, task-related and transactive memory with them. Hence, hotels benefit from encouraged communication and comprehension, building up a stock of shared mental models. These processes are fostered by team structures.

Nevertheless, there is a tradeoff between shared knowledge and the acquisition of new knowledge concerning the hotel chain as a whole. The generation of new knowledge (learning) implies to find distinctions (Luhmann, 1985; Spencer Brown, 1969). High rates of shared mental models hinder distinction making and therefore impede learning speed in hotels. Different mental models (distributed knowledge) instead permit increased distinction making and diverse expert knowledge in hotels. These mechanisms work internally and externally. A high rate of shared (background) knowledge limits the ability to acquire new external knowledge through less specialization. Consequently, distributed task-specific and distributed task-related knowledge needs to be combined with shared task-specific and task-related knowledge in a group of employees. On the other hand, a high rate of shared (background) knowledge fosters the capability to communicate and transfer the knowledge in the hotels. This underlines the relevance of cognitive and behavioral linkages between hotel staff and the existence of shared background knowledge to ensure learning. Shared mental models contain values, norms, beliefs, quality standards, and other background knowledge. Shared background knowledge allows successful communication within hotels and between the single hotels of a hotel chain and with shared quality awareness. A shared language and commonly understood symbols encourage and incorporate shared background knowledge. Shared background knowledge incorporating internalized hotel-wide knowledge helps to interpret other information and knowledge similarity. Hotels in which employees from different countries work face limitations in case of a shared language. Even people who share the same mother tongue can have communication problems due to the ambiguity of language (the same word has different meanings and different topics are defined by dissimilar words). While commonly interpreted words help knowledge's comprehension and distribution, hotels require to build up pieces of shared language. That needs learning the phrases and their usage as they occur by the practice of an organization's language in hotels.

Open and direct communication between employees helps to identify and internalize the concepts and phrases in hotels (see Chapter 6.1.3 (Team Structures)). Reciprocal interactions with care can prevent misunderstanding. Trust bearing relationships and the understanding that language often includes misunderstanding lessens the negative effects of concepts' unshared meanings. Shared values can also promote the democratization of knowledge in order to remove it from "the knowledge is power–and I am the owner" context.

### *Personalized or Codified Knowledge Transfer?*

In personalization strategy, in which people act as knowledge sources, employees accumulate, distribute and transfer knowledge through personal interactions. Personalization's goal often tends to find the most suited expert for a problem in larger or locally distributed hotels. Personalization allows the transfer of tacit knowledge. Thereby, the main use of information technology is to facilitate communication and to ease the retrieval of internal experts. Hence, social processes play a dominant role in personalization.

Knowledge transfer underlies two mechanisms. Firstly, direct interactions allow the perception of different verbal and non-verbal information. Information transfer by telephone, e-mail, and post-mail instead limits knowledge transfer to explicit knowledge. The broader and media richer information and knowledge transfer in personal interaction enables people to interpret the transferred information and knowledge more precisely. So personal and direct communication assists the production of shared distinction making and assists identical knowledge transfer in the case of a specific task. Secondly, the effects of the knowledge transfer become more visible at an earlier time in direct personal interactions. Directly interrelating employees can evaluate gestures, mimics, and actions of each other. This is very important for service processes, in which embedded and tacit knowledge plays a major role. The interacting individuals transfer knowledge and information and intensify distinction making by recursive processes. Associations and the dynamic of speech acts (Searle, 1969; Searle, 1979) foster new insights, which can generate new individual or shared knowledge in hotels and their directly interacting service staff.

Personalization can aim to promote shared models or to enhance the combination of distributed knowledge. To build up an enhanced combination of distributed knowledge, hotels should focus on a better retrieval of expert-knowledge (e.g., experience concerning specific events, conferences, quality programs, service innovations, etc.). Nevertheless, personalization permits shared mental models that guide an identical interpretation of transferred knowledge or allow a direct personal transfer of tacit knowledge. Direct communication, such as can be found in apprenticeships with direct interaction between instructor and trainee, allows the transfer of implicit or process-orientated tacit knowledge (Lave & Wenger, 2000: 169). Additionally practice trials on related problems promote the transfer of tacit knowledge and of specific working skills relevant to the hotel industry. While giving the trainees a chance to observe, imitate and test skills, participative apprenticeships with direct involvement encourage the transfer of implicit knowledge. Imitation also gives opportunities to transfer routines that are relevant tacit knowledge for hotels. However, skill and routine learning is always slow because it needs practice, direct and reciprocal interaction, and a willingness to be temporarily incompetent (Nelson & Winter, 1982: 123; Schein, 1993: 86).

Codification strategy extracts knowledge from the person who generated it, and stores it in databases (Hansen et al., 1999). This enables firms to extract knowledge from persons and to achieve person-independent knowledge that everyone in the firm can retrieve. Codification strategy permits the staff to search for and to retrieve codified knowledge without having contact to the original owner of the knowledge in dispersed hotels. This is very important for hotel chains, when they need to retrieve knowledge developed from experience with others across boundaries of time and space. Hence, information technology plays a significant role in a codification strategy. Nevertheless, codification does not guarantee an identical transfer of knowledge because employees will interpret the "knowledge" (information or connected and goal orientated knowledge) in databases differently due to the subjectivity of individual minds. To interpret and use the codified knowledge in an identical manner, staff has to share some of the other's mental models. Thus, hotel chains require similar or overlapping background knowledge. Background knowledge consists mainly of commonly shared beliefs, values, and language. A common language has strong effects on knowledge transfer, because unshared words cause misunderstandings. The ambiguity of language promotes misunderstanding. Further, the connection and accentuation of words leads to different understandings of a topic. Commonly held aspects of language promote understanding and the quality of knowledge transfer (von Krogh & Roos, 1996: 424). Consequently, a common language improves the fulfillment of (codified) quality standards in hotel chains.

Codification does not only imply putting knowledge into databases. For the improvement of service quality, knowledge has to be used, diversified and distributed in hotels (leveraging of knowledge). The choice of an adequate information technology and database facilitates knowledge transfer. Distributed technologies or intranet sites can effectively spread specific forms of knowledge and information. They also are able to generate virtual forums for connecting specialists (see personalization) and expert knowledge (Cross & Baird, 2000: 71). For codification purposes the databases must contain more structured knowledge than for personalization. Databases concerning a codification strategy store primarily codified experiences (e.g., reports of specific events, best practices in different hotel, the formulation of quality standards, service quality programs, company-wide training courses, operation standards for various services, tourist trend news, etc.).

Organizational artifacts incorporating specific operations and actions complement a codification strategy. These artifacts bear a long-term influence on employees' behavior and establish shared understanding of specific tasks. A prime example of artifacts embedding knowledge (food and restaurant) and bringing it into practice is McDonald's. McDonald's engaged primarily in knowledge by designing machines, which make it virtually impossible to overcook hamburgers, underserve the amount of fries, or shortchange the customer (McGill & Slocum, 1993: 69). Such knowledge structures store knowledge independently from individuals and allow the implementation of rotating staff while limiting failure and determining specific actions and operations. Thus, engineered knowledge is suitable for back-office operations like in restaurants, booking procedures, or cleaning in hotels. They allow the utilization of different unskilled and rotating employees. Nevertheless, hotels' ability to engineer personal service operations with direct customer is limited. Though this interface primarily influences hotel-guests' service evaluation and the implementation of engineered knowledge limits further learning (Cross & Baird, 2000: 76), it is not suitable for non-repetitive operations or more flexible service operations.

Resuming hotels should follow a hybrid strategy of personalization and codification. First, the high rate of implicit process orientated knowledge and skills illustrates the relevance of personalization in hotels. Second, the possibility of intense communication with the customer forces the relevance of personalization strategy in hotels. Direct personal communication facilitates the acquisition of customer-related knowledge and thus enables the hotel to provide an individualized service. Third, employees have to internalize shared values of customer orientation for the need of customer-oriented quality delivery.

## ILLUSTRATIONS OF STRUCTURES
## FOR KNOWLEDGE MANAGEMENT IN HOTELS

### Knowledge Information System

Hotels' employment of people in diverse countries occurs in particular economic, political and social environments, and in hotels with different market conditions and practices (Medlik, 1990: 88). Although different items of a knowledge management system are meaningful, hotels can benefit from an information system and a hotel-wide access to the system. While hotels require personalization and codification, the knowledge information system should allow the retrieval of experts and of codified knowledge (e.g., new meal patterns can be saved in a knowledge information system allowing food services to increase meal variety). Often such systems are defined as groupware or computer-supported cooperative work systems.

Experts, which are motivated communicating their knowledge, have to be found in the intra- or Internet, or Lotus Notes system. The expert-knowledge needs to be categorized and labeled. In order to manage the ambiguity of language and different languages, hotels should create diverse labels for specific topics in the information system. Afterwards, employees can make use of search machines to retrieve the name, address, telephone number, and e-mail of the expert. Especially, e-mail assures a quick communication and the possibility of digital information exchange, but it hinders the transfer of tacit knowledge. Thus, the knowledge information system can lead to personal communication. Knowledge's distribution should not concentrate on e-mail systems. E-mail systems contain specific recipients to whom the knowledge is sent. Employees who are not on the mailing list do not receive potentially useful information. Additionally, the received information might be useless at a certain time, but valuable later. Knowledge distributed via e-mail is decentralized, allowing informal information exchange, but often might be redundant, inconsistent or misleading, if opponent information is distributed. Employees who do not work with computers are excluded from the information system.

Moreover, the Inter- and intranet based knowledge information system should contain codified knowledge about best practice, quality standards, operation standards, characteristics of the geographically distributed hotels, the USP of the region and experts which can provide knowledge for specific topics, and information about customers (preferences, target group membership, etc.). Additionally, the knowledge about customers accumulated in databases encourages increased levels of customization. To provide opportunity to monitor and evaluate information and interpretation of worldwide customers' preferences via the intranet, hotels have to accumulate and save internally and externally acquired knowledge. Some of the customer-orientated knowledge can be achieved via central information and reservation systems. The information systems form the basis for the transfer of the specific customers' preferences between employees in hotels. In addition, the technique of data mining offers hotels an instrument identifying new trends in tourism and hospitality faster and enhances customization. Instead, providing guests with information and acquiring knowledge clients should have a limited access to specific topics of the Internet (special offers, hotels of the chain, characteristics of the destination, etc.) and should be able to communicate with the hotel directly.

The advantages in effectiveness and efficiency a knowledge information system offers depends on the hotel chain's competence to establish knowledge retrieval, accumulation, and distribution in the different hotels. The maintenance and utilization of a knowledge information system requires constant knowledge input. Consequently, hotels need to motivate their staff generating and accumulating valuable knowledge into the database. Though not every bit of knowledge is valuable, hotels should establish responsibilities for knowledge accumulation and maintenance of the system (see knowledge executives). According to the high ratio of unskilled workers in hotels who often have no access to the Inter- and intranet, and operations that do not require the use of a computer for their service operations, hotels need to implement specific knowledge-centered positions and people who identify, distribute, and save the knowledge in information systems. Knowledge officers accumulate and retrieve the knowledge into databases and have to communicate the knowledge to the staff. Moreover, globally acting hotel chains are especially confronted with different languages of customers and staff. The information in the knowledge information system requires hotel-wide comprehension and the selection of worldwide spoken language as a common medium–most probably English as a worldwide language. Although non-native English speakers can have problems with the foreign language and misinterpretations might follow, they can understand most of the content.

Further, some recommendations about a knowledge information system can be emphasized:

- Knowledge has to be structured. The structure of the documents and files limits or allows the utilization of knowledge.
- Workers' task-specific knowledge and experiences should be integrated in databases and systems.
- Knowledge has to be maintained continuously to provide actual knowledge.
- Search engines and intelligent agents should be included for retrieval of specific and often intertwined task-related knowledge.
- Information about the author and experts has to be integrated permitting direct communication and the transfer of tacit knowledge.

Hotels, in which information systems and data mining techniques are implemented, can also suffer from insufficient knowledge management. Employees do not use the knowledge that is acquired externally or internally and accumulated in databanks because:

- they might not realize the benefits of the systems,
- they might have no access to computers,
- they might not be able to transform codified knowledge into service operations,
- they might not internalize the gathered know-how or know-why, or
- find experts that are not motivated to answer their questions, etc.

Hotels can implement a number of structures to enhance the utilization and the motivation of the knowledge management, which are displayed in Chapters 6.1.2 (Knowledge Executives), 6.1.3 (Team Structures), and 6.1.4 (Knowledge Circles).

The German Hotel group Maritim has more than 40 first-class hotels in Germany, Teneriffa, and Mauritius. Maritim hotels concentrates on the distribution of guest-related knowledge via information technologies. With a recently introduced guest card that contains all accumulated information about clients the hotels are enabled to prepare for guests' preferences. Since Maritim hotels get information about the guests at the point of booking, they can plan guest specific service operations in advance. Thereby, Maritim hotels can reduce the number of service operations in the front office and check-in is accelerated. During the guests' hotel stay, service staff acquire and accumulate new information about the guests to provide superior service quality for future trips. Besides, Maritim group and single hotels use the data from guests cards for differentiated target group marketing, mailings, etc., and benefit from the comfortable and uncomplicated guest card system. The guest card gives every guest a higher status without status differences, which can discriminate other clients. Guests collect discounts in Euro on all expenditures in the hotels. Lacking block-out dates, guests are able to refund money any time during their check-out.

*Knowledge Executives*

Although the basis of knowledge management is provided by motivated employees, they have to be supported with structural aspects and leadership. Top management's commitment to knowledge management and the organization of strategies, and programs can be underlined by the position of a chief knowledge officer. As hotel chains have to generate knowledge incessantly, they require a knowledge vision, which harmonizes knowledge management throughout the different hotels. The chief knowledge officer's role is to articulate the knowledge vision and goals and communicate it throughout the whole hotel chain. Therefore, the chief knowledge officer defines knowledge goals, knowledge strategies, knowledge controlling, and is responsible for the structure of the hotel-wide information system. A knowledge department is responsible for some functions to be centralized, e.g., training programs and develops the infrastructure for the information technology. Although knowledge management requires decentralization and motivated employees, the department is necessary because a widespread hotel chain needs specialized knowledge services and the complexity of an information system has to be managed. The knowledge department ensures global consistency of the databases, and periodically reviews and updates knowledge assets (e.g., best practices, trends in tourism, benchmarks). Content manager(s) or web gardener(s) maintain the design and data in the information system. The knowledge department assists the hotels to plan meetings between experts and knowledge officers who work in the hotel.

Knowledge officers who work in the hotels but communicate with the knowledge department provide the link between hotels and the centralized information system. They serve as a bridge between the goals and visions of the chief knowledge officer and the often chaotic and complex service operations in the hotels. Knowledge officers break down the visions, goals, and programs into concepts that diverse service personnel can understand and implement in their operations. As knowledge officers communicate intensively vertical, horizontal, and with guests they contribute to a bottom up approach in knowledge management. So they act as gatekeepers. Gatekeepers are organizations' members, who engage heavily in the accumulation, transmission, and absorption of internal and external knowledge in a firm (Leonard, 1995: 157). As socio-metric stars, they monitor the environment for new knowledge and communicate the acquired knowledge in the organization (Allen, 1977; Katz & Tushmann, 1981). The knowledge officer assists all workers and normally co-ordinate the knowledge work of the specialist departments in a hotel. Via leadership they strengthen the motivation and ability of workers to contribute to the knowledge base and distribute knowledge. They also plan meetings between employees (waiter in a hotel or different hotels) and organize knowledge circles or knowledge teams, in which tacit and explicit knowledge can be distributed. In these meetings or circles a decentralized knowledge system develops that sustains informal communication.

The direct communication, which knowledge officers promote hotel-wide, allows a fast transfer and distribution of gained knowledge in the hotel. The diverse cultural and functional backgrounds of hotels' employees additionally require diverse, culturally-skilled knowledge officers, which can build-up linkages between existent knowledge and new knowledge during knowledge transfer.

Knowledge officers have the authority and responsibility to maintain knowledge and to modify the decentralized contents of the knowledge database, e.g., the hotel's intra- and internet. Since the loss of a single knowledge officer could cause a dramatic knowledge drain, a team of knowledge officers is advisable. The knowledge officer is also engaged in meetings with other hotels' knowledge officers to facilitate the identification, development, and retrieval of knowledge. The hotels' knowledge officers' team has to communicate and interrelate intensively with employees to absorb and/or to distribute knowledge.

Maritim hotels enhance knowledge distribution by face-to-face meetings between executives and with staff. Thereby Maritim increases the transfer of tacit and explicit knowledge improving a transactive memory system and task-related or task-specific knowledge. Figure 2 illustrates the different participants of the meetings.

*Team Structures*

Although hotels have implemented different techniques like guest cards and have acquired customer related know-what the knowledge is not distributed in different hotels nor internalized by hotel staff. Conse-

FIGURE 2. Knowledge Transfer in Maritim Hotels

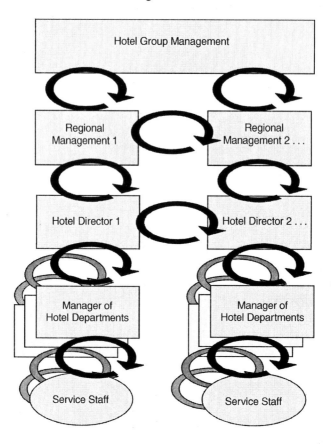

quently, besides to marketing techniques (data mining) and information systems and knowledge officers, hotels should further implement team structures and inter-team meetings, which allow knowledge transfer and the internalization of knowledge. A hotel's ability to benefit from external knowledge lies in the employees who embody the interface between the firm and its external environment (e.g., tourist office, government, guests). Finally, they are responsible for the transfer of attained knowledge between subunits and employees of the hotel. On the one hand, hotels require staff, which are able to absorb customer-oriented knowledge and distribute it throughout the organization. Such tasks demand the ability to identify and develop new ideas. Generally, companies that are successful at generating new ideas have porous organizations developed around structures like contact centers, permitting maximum knowledge transfer and avoiding endless approvals and communication delays (Quinn, 2000: 24). Moreover, flat organizations promote individual responsibility and flexibility, which are critical to fast response, highly motivated to find new opportunities (Quinn, 2000: 24). On the other hand, tacit and explicit knowledge from other hotels has to be implemented in operations, which often happen under direct customer interrelations through the service encounter. Some of the explicit and tacit knowledge needs to be shared; some of the knowledge is distributed. Nevertheless, incremental reciprocal processes foster the transfer of tacit knowledge and improve shared knowledge. Information sharing, networking, and information relationship building generally take place at social functions, and meetings of professional groups of different hotel professionals (Rutherford & Umbreit, 1994: 330f.). Consequently, hotels have to promote open structures and team-based operations together with the establishment of flat organization structures that are in the minority in hotel business, today. On top of that, while work experiences can act as an extremely powerful mechanism to ensure effective knowledge generation and implementation, executives should promote the learning ability and the knowledge transfer in hotels. Whereas tacit knowledge plays a dominant role in service operations, hotels should focus on teams.

Hotels ought to arrange teams of staff concerned with similar tasks in order to develop shared task-specific knowledge. Such teams act as powerful wells of knowledge, generating, identifying, promoting, developing and distributing knowledge through direct interrelations. This is especially valid for the transfer of tacit knowledge and the evolution of shared mental models. First, teams allow a sense of reciprocity and trust building up over time. This social relationship improves better cognitive understanding, expectations, and mutual understanding permitting functional relationships for future tasks. Second, the enriched understanding of the others knowledge and skills improves the task fulfillment by the amplification of team related knowledge and evolving shared norms, values, and beliefs. Especially hotel staff, which interacts constantly with guests, cannot engage in knowledge transfer completely; they have to prosecute operations. Prosecuting operations in team structures promotes learning through observation and imitation. Moreover, training the individual task-fulfillment allows through the direct contact the transfer of explicit and tacit knowledge. Moreover, training the individual task-fulfillment allows the transfer of explicit and tacit knowledge through the direct contact and permit the transfer of service operations and routines.

Even knowledge transfer to lesser skilled employees in a specific topic requires considerable effort and time. This especially holds valid for training on the job while starting on trivial tasks before moving on to tasks that are more complex. Therefore, teams are better capable of developing and distributing new knowledge about customers by discourse and customer interrelation whilst carrying out operations. Additionally the staff's closeness to guests fosters the absorption of customer-related knowledge. Taking time to reflect on experiences, and thus, to define what is learned encourages experience-based knowledge generation. Employees that are engaged in business operations often use and absorb implicit knowledge, which limits the articulation of knowledge in hotels. Therefore, direct interaction with other employees is crucial.

Moreover, most staff with direct customer contact have limited access to information technology, experience with computers, and time for data processing (e.g., restaurant staff) so that other knowledge workers (e.g., gatekeepers or knowledge officers) should be obliged to absorb the staff's knowledge, integrate it into databases and furthermore provide the staff with new knowledge from the database.

*Knowledge Circles*

Hotels have to secure knowledge identification, generation, accumulation, and transfer. Personal communication between staff and between executives and staff allows the exchange of tacit and explicit knowledge. Because the patriarchal and authoritarian leadership style of hotel's executives sanctions open knowledge transfer, knowledge management orientated leadership and empowerment has to be established and hierarchical boundaries minimized in hotels. Knowledge generation starts with empowered employees, who are able to identify and solve problems and new ideas as well as to discuss them openly. Therefore, hotels implement knowledge circles that are under control of the hotels' knowledge officer. Knowledge circles are institutionalized sessions between employees that enable members to discuss problems, challenges and new insights, similar to quality circles organization.

Knowledge circles also promote the transfer of knowledge allowing horizontal and open communication. For the improvement of communication, hotels require common background knowledge. Knowledge circles transfer knowledge through staff's discourse of new ideas and of problems with customers. Specific topics (e.g., guests' complaints or changing customer preferences) for each session promote the discourse and improve knowledge transfer. Input from Top Management into knowledge circles about new challenges in the environment, in the hotel chain, and in the region can also promote learning in the hotel. Allowing hotel-wide retrieval of the generated knowledge, the knowledge officers or his assistants can also integrate the new knowledge into the knowledge management information system.

## CASE STUDY

The Accor hotel group (worldwide 3,500 hotels, 130,000 employees, brands like Formula One, Ibis, Novotel, Sofitel) is considering and establishing a wide-ranging knowledge management system in Germany where Accor has 6,000 employees. The knowledge management system is based on three stakes:

1. IT-based knowledge accumulation
2. access to the IT-based knowledge system
3. motivation for knowledge utilization and generation.

The Accor hotel group is engaged in the formulation of knowledge goals. An Internet-based intranet will be improved, which contains data about best practice, service innovations, and training possibilities. The intranet also contains tool-like flight plans or train schedules to allow easier fulfillment of guests' wishes and requirements. Business TV channels in which Accor supplies films and information allow the transfer of tacit and implicit knowledge. Generated knowledge is accumulated in databases and in persons. The German head office is looking for a knowledge manager, who is responsible for the infrastructure of a knowledge management system. The different departments in the head office work on the decentralized knowledge management system, although the specialized departments provide a high proportion of the knowledge management's content. Besides, knowledge for the knowledge base will be acquired internally from the hotels and their service personnel. Search engines provide the retrieval of knowledge, which is codified and labeled. Knowledge can be retrievable according to the employees' status. Therefore, computers will be installed in lounges to provide Internet access to employees, who do not need computers for their operations. For motivation purposes, idea contests, bonuses, benchmarks, etc., are installed and the knowledge management system is easy to handle. The implementation of knowledge management profits from the open corporate culture and decentralization. Decentralization additionally supports different levels and applications of knowledge management in diverse countries. Besides, between service staff in different hotels informal networks exists. New practices can be generated and tested by hotel directors' prototyping. Successful practices can be implemented in more hotels.

Moreover, Accor improves knowledge by human resource training and knowledge circles to improve service quality in the service encounter. Knowledge circles and projects concerning specific goals especially in the field of service operations, which concentrate on task-specific knowledge, are established throughout the hotel group. Training and knowledge circles are also concerned with the implementation of the knowledge management system. Training programs and knowledge circles increase the transactive memory and lead to meetings between experts, who are able to exchange tacit and explicit knowledge.

## CONCLUSION

This article stresses the role knowledge plays as a main source for quality improvements and competitive advantages in hotels, urging them to implement knowledge management. Especially, the direct customer interface, the high ratio of low status employees, the high rate of staff fluctuation and rotation, the dispersed single hotels of a hotel chain, which face different environmental effects, and the need for global and hotel-wide quality standards require a specific knowledge management designed for hotels. The paper contributes to knowledge management and hotel management literature. It presents reflections about knowledge and knowledge management in hotels based on theoretical considerations about individual and organizational knowledge that can incorporate shared or distributed mental organizational models.

Although some elements of a knowledge management system can be more dominant than others, hotels should realize that knowledge management is a system of interacting parts. Although knowledge management represents an integrated system, this paper lays a focus on knowledge strategies and structural aspects, because they strongly differ from other industries' requirements.

A knowledge strategy concerns the type of organizational knowledge (shared or distributed) and the type of knowledge transfer (personalization or codification). Shared mental models enhance work coordination and minimize knowledge drain when single workers leave the hotel. Hotel chains benefit from shared mental models because these promote work coordination, understanding, and the effectiveness of communication throughout the different hotels. Distributed mental models improve work specialization, which hotels also require when establishing high-quality standards. Shared mental models are especially advisable for held norms, values, and beliefs hotel-wide and in working teams. Distributed models are mostly suited for the different task-specific knowledge of different working teams and for task-related knowledge in teams, because they allow for specialization and variety of knowledge. Diverse knowledge promotes distinction making, which in turn encourages the development of new knowledge. Thus, hotels should concentrate more on their absorptive capacity, which contains the integration of customer knowledge representing a major source for knowledge development through the service encounter. Often codification and personalization are seen as opposing knowledge strategies. For hotels, a hybrid strategy is advisable since some tacit knowledge and skills (embedded service routines) can only be transferred in direct personal relationships, which are widespread in the hotel-business. Additionally, codified knowledge is required to retrieve and distribute knowledge in the globally dispersed hotels of a hotel chain.

The implementation of knowledge management benefits from knowledge executives, knowledge information system, and team structures. A knowledge information system shapes the technical basis for the accumulation, retrieval, and distribution of explicit knowledge or facilitates the finding of experts company-wide. A system of knowledge executives provides responsibility for knowledge management. Additionally leadership helps to motivate knowledge workers and knowledge orientation in hotels. Team structures and knowledge circles that promote the personalized transfer of tacit and explicit knowledge assist the implementation of a knowledge management system. In the end, knowledge management should promote some democratization of knowledge in order to remove it from the "knowledge is power–and I am the owner" context.

While the paper identifies and discusses distinctive characteristics of knowledge management in hotels and gives advice, it has certain limitations. Specific items of hotels' management systems, which could not be discussed here due to the complexity of the concept, can be examined more deeply. Especially, the interactions between various relationships (single hotel to head office, single hotel to single hotel, and hotels to customers) and that the results should be closely scrutinized. The same holds for the diverse cultural influences a specific hotel chain is subject to. Therefore, further studies should concentrate on specific items on knowledge management in hotels by expanding the findings of this article.

## REFERENCES

Allen, T. J. (1977). *Managing the Flow of Technology Transfer to Developing Countries and the Dissemination of Technological Information Within the R&D Organization*. Cambridge, MA: MIT Press.

Badaracco, J. L. (1991). *The Knowledge Link–How Firms Compete Through Strategic Alliances*. Boston, MA: Harvard Business School Press.

Banks, A. P., & Millward, L. J. (2000). Running Shared Mental Models as a Distributed Cognitive Process. *British Journal of Psychology, 91*(4), 513-523.

Boisot, M. H. (1998). *Knowledge Assets. Securing Competitive Advantage in the Information Economy*. New York: Oxford University Press.

Cannon, M. D., & Edmondson, A. C. (2001). Confronting Failure: Antecedents and Consequences of Shared Beliefs About Failure in Organizational Work Groups. *Journal of Organizational Behavior, 22*(2), 161-178.

Cannon-Bowers, J. A., & Salas, E. (2001). Reflections on Shared Cognition. *Journal of Organizational Behavior, 22*(2), 195-202.

Cannon-Bowers, J. A., Salas, E., & Converse, S. (1993). Shared Mental Models in Team Decision Making. In J. N. Castellan (Ed.), *Individual and Group Decision Making* (Vol. 22, pp. 221-246). Hillsdale, New Jersey: Lawrence Erlbaum Associates.

Cannon-Bowers, J. A., Tannenbaum, S., Salas, E., & Volpe, C. E. (1995). Defining Team Competencies and Establishing Team Training Requirements. In R. Guzzo & E. Salas (Eds.), *Team Effectiveness and Decision Making in Organizations* (pp. 330-380). San Francisco: Jossey-Bass.

Carley, K. M. (1997). Extracting Team Mental Models Through Textual Analysis. *Journal of Organizational Behavior, 18*(3), 533-558.

Cohen, W. M., & Levinthal, D. A. (1990). Absorptive Capacity: A New Perspective on Learning and Innovation. *Administrative Science Quarterly, 35*(1), 128-152.

Cross, R., & Baird, C. (2000). Feeding Organizational Memory: Improving on Knowledge Management's Promise to Business Performance. In R. Cross & S. B. Israelit (Eds.), *Strategic Learning in a Knowledge Economy: Individual, Collective, and Organizational Learning Process*. Woburn, MA: Butterworth-Heinemann.

Drucker, P. (1999). *Management Challenges for the 21st Century*. New York: Harper & Row.

Drucker, P., Dyson, E., Handy, C., Saffo, P., & Senge, P. (1997). Looking Ahead: Implications of the Present. *Harvard Business Review, 75*(5), 18-35.

Fallon, P., & Schofield, P. (2000). Service Quality Measurement and Triadic Interaction: A Comparative Analysis of Stakeholder Perspectives Using TRIQUEST. *Journal of Quality Assurance in Hospitality & Tourism, 1*(3), 29-47.

Fitzsimmons, J. A., & Fitzsimmons, M. J. (1994). *Service Management for Competitive Advantage*. Singapore: McGraw-Hill.

Grant, M. (1996). Toward a Knowledge-based Theory of the Firm. *Strategic Management Journal, 17* (Winter Special Issue), 109-122.

Hansen, M. T., Nohria, N., & Tierney, T. (1999). What's Your Strategy for Managing Knowledge? *Harvard Business Review, 77*(2), 106-118.

Heffner, T. S., Mathieu, J. E., & Cannon-Bowers, J. A. (1995). *The Impact on Shared Mental Models on Team Performance. Sharedness, Quality or Both?* Paper presented at the Symposium Annual Meeting of the Society for Industrial and Organizational Psychology.

Heffner, T. S., Mathieu, J. E., & Goodwin, G. F. (1998). *Team Training: The Impact on Shared Mental Models on Team Performance.* Paper presented at the Symposium Annual Meeting of the Society for Industrial and Organizational Psychology, Dallas, Texas.

Johnson-Laird, P. (1983). *Mental Models.* Cambridge, MA: Harvard University Press.

Katz, R., & Tushmann, M. L. (1981). An Investigation into the Managerial Roles and Career Path of Gatekeepers and Project Supervisors in a Major R&D Facility. *R&D Management, 11*(3), 103-110.

Keiser, J. R. (1989). *Principles and Practices of Management in the Hospitality Industry.* (2 ed.). New York: Van Nostrand Reinhold.

Kim, D. H. (1993). The Link between Individual and Organizational Learning. *Sloan Management Review, 35*(1), 37-50.

Lane, P. J., & Lubatkin, M. (1998). Relative Capacity and Interorganizational Learning. *Strategic Management Journal, 19*(5), 461-477.

Lathi, R. (2000). Knowledge Transfer and Management Consulting: A Look at "The Firm." *Business Horizons, 43*(1), 65-74.

Lave, J., & Wenger, E. (2000). Legitimate Peripheral Participation in Communities of Practice. In R. Cross & S. Israelit (Eds.), *Strategic Learning in a Knowledge Economy: Individual, Collective, and Organizational Learning Process* (pp. 167-184). Woburn, MA: Butterworth-Heinemann.

Leonard, D. (1995). *Wellsprings of Knowledge. Building and Sustaining the Sources of Innovation.* Boston, MA: Harvard Business School Press.

Leonard, D., & Sensiper, S. (1998). The Role of Tacit Knowledge in Group Innovation. *California Management Review, 40*(3), 112-128.

Luhmann, N. (1985). *Social Systems.* Stanford: Stanford University Press.

Luhmann, N. (2000). *Art as a Social System.* Stanford: Stanford University Press.

Lyles, M. (1994). The Impact of Organizational Learning on Joint Venture Formations. *International Business Review, 3*(4), 459-467.

Marchant, D. A., Kettinger, W. J., & Rollins, J. D. (2000). Information Orientation: People, Technology and the Bottom Line. *Sloan Management Review, 41*(4), 69-80.

McGill, M., & Slocum, J. (1993). Unlearning the Organization. *Organizational Dynamics, 22*(3), 67-79.

Medlik, S. (1990). *The Business of Hotels* (2 ed.). Oxford: Heinemann.

Mir, R., & Watson, A. (2000). Strategic Management and the Philosophy Science: The Case for a Constructivist Methodology. *Strategic Management Journal, 21*(9), 941-953.

Mohammed, S., Klimoski, R., & Rentsch, J. (2000). The Measurement of Team Mental Models: We have no Shared Schema. *Organizational Research Models, 3*(2), 123-165.

Nelson, R., & Winter, S. (1982). *An Evolutionary Theory of Economic Change* (Vol. 4). Cambridge, MA, London: Belknap Press of Harvard University Press.

Nightingale, M. (1985). The Hospitality Industry: Defining Quality for a Quality Assurance Program–A Study of Perceptions. *Service Industries Journal, 5*(1), 9-22.

Nonaka, I. (1991). The Knowledge-Creating Company. *Harvard Business Review, 69*(Nov.-Dec.), 96-104.

Nonaka, I., Byosiere, P., Borucki, C. C., & Konno, N. (1994). Organizational Knowledge Creation Theory: A First Comprehensive Test. *International Business Review, 3*(4), 337-351.

Nonaka, I., & Tageuchi, H. (1995). *The Knowledge-Creating Company.* New York: Oxford University Press.

Polanyi, M. (1967). *The Tacit Dimension.* New York: Doubleday.

Post, G. (1999). *Knowledge Management in Management Consulting Firms.* Paper presented at the International ISMICK Symposium: Knowledge Management: Enterprise, Network, and Learning, Compiegne.

Powers, T. (1995). *Introduction to Management in the Hospitality Industry* (5 ed.). New York: Wiley.

Quinn, J. B. (2000). Outsourcing Information: The New Engine of Growth. *Sloan Management Review, 41*(4), 13-28.

Rentsch, J. R., Heffner, T. S., & Duffy, L. T. (1994). What Do You Know Is What You Get from Experience. *Group and Organization Management, 19*(4), 450-474.

Rutherford, D. G., & Umbreit, T. G. (1994). Improving Interactions Between Meeting Planners and Hotel Employees. In D. G. Rutherford (Ed.), *Hotel Management and Operations* (pp. 320-338). New York, etc.: Van Nostrand Reinhold.

Schein, E. H. (1993). How Can Organizations Learn Faster? The Challenge of Entering the Green Room. *Sloan Management Review, 34*(2), 85-92.

Schreinemakers (Ed.) (1999). *Advances in Knowledge Management.* Rotterdam: Ergon.

Searle, J. R. (1969). *Speech Acts: An Essay in the Philosophy Language.* London: Cambridge University Press.

Searle, J. R. (1979). *Expression and Meaning: Studies in the Theory of Speech Acts.* New York: Cambridge University Press.

Seely Brown, J., & Duguid, P. (1998). Organizing Knowledge. *California Management Review, 40*(3), 90-111.

Senge, P. M. (1990). *The Fifth Discipline. The Art and Practice of the Learning Organization.* New York: Doubleday.

Spencer Brown, G. (1969). *Laws of Form.* London: Allen Unwin.

Spender, J. C. (1994). Organizational Knowledge, Collective Practice and Penrose Rents. *International Business Review, 3*(4), 353-367.

Stout, R. J., Cannon-Bowers, J. A., Salas, E., & Milanovic, D. M. (1999). Cognitive Processes-Planning, Shared Mental Models, and Coordinated Performance: An Empirical Link Is Established. *Human factors, 41*(1), 61-71.

Teare, R., Mazanec, J. A., Crawford-Welch, S., & Calver, S. (1994). *Marketing in Hospitality and Tourism*. London, New York: Casell.

Teece, D. J. (1984). Capturing Value from Knowledge Assets: The New Economy, Markets for Know-How, and Intangible Assets. *California Management Review*, *40*(3), 55-79.

Tsoukas, H. (1996). The Firm as a Distributed Knowledge System: A Constructionist Approach. *Strategic Management Journal*, *17* (Winter Special Issue), 11-25.

Van den Bosch, F. A. J., Volberda, W. H., & de Boer, M. (1999). Coevolution of Forms Absorptive Capacity and Knowledge Environment: Organizational Forms and Combinative Capabilities. *Organization Science*, *10*(5), 551-568.

von Foerster, H. (1984). Principles of Self Organizations in an Socio-Managerial Context. In H. Ulrich & J. B. Probst (Eds.), *Self-Organization and Management of Social Systems* (pp. 2-24). Berlin.

von Foerster, H. (1998). Entdecken oder Erfinden. Wie lässt sich Verstehen? In H. Gummin & H. Meier (Eds.), *Einführung in den Konstruktivismus* (Vol. 4, pp. 41-89). München, Zürich: Piper.

von Glasersfeld, E. (1997). *Radical Constructivism. A Way of Knowing and Learning*. London: Falmer Press.

von Glasersfeld, E. (1998). Konstruktion der Wirklichkeit und des Begriffs der Objektivität. In H. Gummin & H. Meier (Eds.), *Einführung in den Konstruktivismus* (Vol. 4, pp. 9-40). München, Zürich: Piper.

von Krogh, G., & Roos, J. (1996). Five Claims on Knowledge. *European Management Journal*, *14*(4), 423-426.

von Krogh, G., Roos, J., & Slocum, K. (1994). An Essay on Corporate Epistemology. *Strategic Management Journal*, *15* (Special Issue), 53-71.

Wegner, D. M. (1987). Transactive Memory: A Contemporary Analysis of the Group Mind. In B. Mullen & G. R. Goethals (Eds.), *Theories of Group Behavior* (pp. 185-208 (Chapter 9)). New York: Springer.

Young, C. B., & McCuiston, V. E. (2000). Knowledge Management: Innovative Strategies for the Twenty-First Century. In R. Berndt (Ed.), *Innovatives Management.* (pp. 313-325). Berlin: Springer.

# Knowledge Supply Chain Matrix Approach for Balanced Knowledge Management: An Airline Industry Firm Case

Marcel Hattendorf

**SUMMARY.** Knowledge management projects suffer from concepts which overemphasize a single factor, e.g., information technology. This single factor frequently dominates other factors as processes, structures or strategies. The research question of the paper is how to develop and apply a knowledge management tool that balances different factors in knowledge management projects. The introduced tool, called knowledge supply chain matrix, is derived from a generic business model and four knowledge management processes. The paper describes how the tool is applied within a knowledge management project in the airline industry. *[Article copies available for a fee from The Haworth Document Delivery Service: 1-800-HAWORTH. E-mail address: <docdelivery@haworthpress.com> Website: <http://www.HaworthPress. com> © 2002 by The Haworth Press, Inc. All rights reserved.]*

**KEYWORDS.** Balanced knowledge management, knowledge supply chain matrix, airline industry

Marcel Hattendorf is affiliated with the Arthur D. Little International GmbH, Palais Todesco, Kärntner Strasse 51, A-1015 Wien, Austria (E-mail: hattendorf.marcel@adlittle.com).

[Haworth co-indexing entry note]: "Knowledge Supply Chain Matrix Approach for Balanced Knowledge Management: An Airline Industry Firm Case." Hattendorf, Marcel. Co-published simultaneously in *Journal of Quality Assurance in Hospitality & Tourism* (The Haworth Hospitality Press, an imprint of The Haworth Press, Inc.) Vol. 3, No. 3/4, 2002, pp. 61-73; and: *Knowledge Management in Hospitality and Tourism* (ed: Ricarda B. Bouncken and Sungsoo Pyo) The Haworth Hospitality Press, an imprint of The Haworth Press, Inc., 2002, pp. 61-73. Single or multiple copies of this article are available for a fee from The Haworth Document Delivery Service [1-800-HAWORTH, 9:00 a.m. - 5:00 p.m. (EST). E-mail address: docdelivery@haworthpress. com].

## INTRODUCTION

Knowledge management initiatives sometimes fail. The paper assumes that the failure is due to inappropriate tools. There is wide variety of knowledge management concepts in the literature. However, the concepts and their tools balance business factors (strategy, core processes, organization and resources) insufficiently. The research question therefore is, how to develop and apply a knowledge management tool that balances business factors.

The paper is divided into two parts. The first part develops the knowledge supply chain matrix as a knowledge management tool. It is due to a business model (high performance business model) and four generic knowledge processes (knowledge generation, knowledge storing, knowledge transfer/application and knowledge measurement) that span a matrix. The matrix represents the knowledge supply chain matrix.

The second part describes the application of the knowledge supply chain matrix in a case study. The company offers services for airlines concerning revenue accounting. The question is how to link business processes with knowledge supply chain matrix so as to structure knowledge management project.

## THE THEORETICAL BACKGROUND

The theoretical background for the knowledge management model is due to the "fit"-idea (Ansoff, 1979; Chandler, 1962), which is still popular in the strategic management field (Bea & Haas, 2001: 9 f.). The "fit"-idea basically says that different business factors as strategy, organization or IT should be aligned in order to work efficiently. As the business environment permanently demands new requirements, it is an ongoing task to line up and adjust the interdependencies among business factors. A well-known business model that is built upon the "fit"-idea is the 7-S model of the consultants Waterman and Peters (Waterman & Peters & Phillips, 1980; Waterman & Peters, 1982) that encompasses seven business factors. They are divided into three "hard" (structure, strategy, systems) and four "soft" (shard values, style, staff, skills) factors. "Hard" factors can be analyzed, designed and controlled, but the management of "soft" factors is relatively limited. Nonetheless, it is the goal to align and balance all of them.

An example for the "fit"-idea in knowledge management is Arthur D. Little's knowledge management concept which consists of four integrated factors or dimensions: content/context, culture, process and infrastructure (Arthur D. Little, 1999; Bergmann, 1999: 34 f.; Bock, 1998: 5 f.). Content and context answer the question which knowledge is relevant for the business. Strategically relevant knowledge has to be identified and evaluated. Knowledge management projects frequently underestimate the meaning of cultural dimensions, e.g., employees are reluctant to share their knowledge. Hence, to promote knowledge transfer in terms of benefit programs might be an appropriate instrument to support change policies. The process dimension pursues to implement organizational processes in order to support the knowledge management activities, for instance by designing an organizational structure in terms of knowledge stewards, knowledge officers, etc. The infrastructure dimension provides the adequate technology so as to support processes in the knowledge management framework. Questions about appropriate tools for capturing data or databases for storing knowledge need to be responded.

## THE HIGH PERFORMANCE BUSINESS MODEL AS CONCEPTUAL STARTING POINT

The knowledge management approach in this paper is due to Arthur D. Little's high performance business model (Arthur D. Little, 1991, 1995: p. 203 f.) (see Figure 1) with its "fit"-idea. This model consists of four factors: strategy, core processes, organization and resources.

Strategy describes the relationship between external and internal stakeholders as customers, employees and shareholders. However, in the context of knowledge management the factor strategy is used in a slightly different manner. Strategy serves in two directions: first, it matches external requirements from the business environment against the products and services provided by the enterprise (inter-"fit"-idea). Secondly, IT matches all internal factors of the enterprise against each other (intra-"fit"-idea) (Bea & Haas, 2001: p. 15).

The factor organization in the high performance model describes the processes and structures supporting critical core processes within the knowledge management. From a process-centric viewpoint it is pertinent to design the process framework as a separate process model with different levels of detail for each core process at the beginning. Then, a knowledge management structure in terms of process owners should be assigned.

The third factor includes HR, IT and financial resources. This paper sets priority on IT aspects. Information technology plays a more passive part within the framework as the technology is regarded as an "enabler" for organizational requirements. This point of view presumes a perspective from the market to the enterprise which can be named as an outside-in or market-based view (Porter, 1980, 1985). Product-market concepts define the strategies for generating competitive advantages for which internal processes, structures and resources have to be aligned. On the other hand, the inside-out or resource-based view regards the market from the enterprise and tries to exploit internal resources for generating competitive advantages beyond market constraints. This perspective provides several variations; the most popular is probably the concept of core competencies (Hamel & Prahalad, 1990, 1994).

The last factor illustrates the core processes which occupy a significant position within the entire knowledge management framework. The core processes serve as the blueprint so as to structure all other factors. Strategy, organization and resources have to be aligned according to the structure and arrangement of core processes. The management literature supplies a variety of propositions for core processes in knowledge management (Mandl, 2001; Mandl & Reinmann-Rothmeier, 2000; Probst & Romhardt, 1997; Romhardt, 1998; Güldenberg, 1998). A well-known approach is due to Davenport/Prusak (Davenport & Prusak, 1998) who recommends three core processes: knowledge generation, knowledge codification and knowledge transfer. However, the knowledge management concept for this paper suggests four slightly different core processes: knowledge generation, knowledge storing, knowledge transfer/application and knowledge measurement. These core processes do not build necessarily a consecutive chain (Romhardt, 1998), but they need to be addressed in order to set-up a holistic knowledge management framework.

Knowledge generation describes the content that is relevant for the entire knowledge management concept. The core process pursues to make internal knowledge assets explicit in order to plan and design content. Knowledge storing illustrates which content needs to be hold and how. For instance, the process has to respond questions about indexing and structuring knowledge assets. Knowledge transfer and application concentrate on the distribution and usage of stored knowledge. Which knowledge has to be provided, to whom and when is a typical subject in this core process. Knowledge measurement assesses the previous core processes with the purpose to draw inferences for the knowledge management design.

FIGURE 1. The High Performance Business Model (*Management der Lernprozessee im Unternehmen.* Wiesbaden. Arthur D. Little, 1995: p. 209)

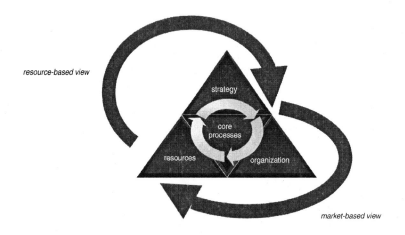

## THE KNOWLEDGE SUPPLY CHAIN MATRIX AS GENERIC KNOWLEDGE MANAGEMENT MODEL

How to apply the High Performance Business Model with its "fit"-idea and the introduced core processes in knowledge management?

The basic picture can be understood as a 2-dimensional matrix that is spanned by both the factors of the High Performance Business Model and the core processes (see also Hattendorf, 2002). That means the factors strategy (content), organization and resources (IT) build the vertical axis and the four core processes describe for the horizontal axis in the matrix. The matrix illustrates the model requirement that strategy, organization and resources are aligned by the core processes. The matrix, called the knowledge supply chain matrix (see Figure 2), creates a pattern with sixteen fields that have to be addressed to knowledge management projects. For instance, for the core process knowledge generation the following questions must be answered:

- Which knowledge must be generated (factor strategy)?
- How to design the process in detail (factor process) and who is in charge for this process (factor structure)?
- Which resources or information technology can support the core process efficiently?

The "fit"-idea demands to line up core processes, strategy, organization and resources in order to define a balanced concept of knowledge management. This approach provides a remarkable benefit in comparison to other concepts: knowledge management initiatives frequently deliver disappointing results as the meaning of one factor, often information technology, is overestimated. The installation of dedicated knowledge management databases with fancy access and reporting tools is insufficient for a holistic knowledge management. Consequently, these projects fail because subjects concerning content or processes are not fully addressed. Hence, a balanced approach, that take into account various factors, might promise a more beneficial method.

## A KNOWLEDGE MANAGEMENT CASE STUDY IN THE AIRLINE INDUSTRY

### Situation

The company is a successful player within the airline industry. Being part of an established airline formerly, the company acts today as an autonomous enterprise for airline revenue accounting. Nonetheless, the

FIGURE 2. The Knowledge Supply Chain Matrix

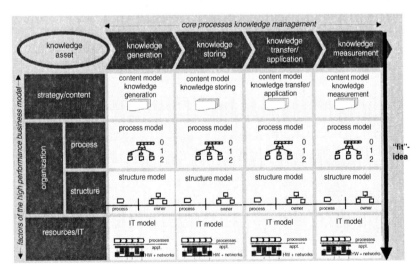

relationship between the former parent company and the former subsidiary are still intensive, so that the main fraction of overall revenue is due to the former parent company. At the end of the nineties the total income was about 50 Mill. US $ with 600 employees.

In sum the company's business model is about cleaning, matching and assessing data streams from various sources which are distributed among different airlines afterwards (see Figure 3). Hence, three generic processes basically encompass the entire value chain: upstream, production and downstream. The upstream process is divided into three data inflows.

1. The "Interline" inflow delivers invoice data from other airlines; e.g., when a passenger buys a flight ticket in order to travel form Vienna to New York via Frankfurt with Austrian Airlines. However, American Airlines transports the passengers from Frankfurt to New York instead of Austrian Airlines, then American Airlines sends an invoice to Austrian Airlines concerning the transport service.
2. Flight tickets are sold by airline-owned or independent ticket agencies. The "Sales" inflow transfers information from ticket agencies to the company either via IT-based channels or manually.
3. Before passengers get on the plane, they have to show their flight ticket at the boarding counter. Parts of the flight ticket are collected by the airport staff and physically sent to the company where high-end scanners read and convert the information from the flight tickets. This process called "Uplift" inflow.

The main task of the company is to manage the upstream process with its three data inflows. However, the delivered information is frequently insufficient or incomplete, so that several processes in the production process check, clean and fix bits of information. Accurate information is a prerequisite for successful flight coupon assessment which is the major outcome of the production core process. The assessment, called "prorating," is due to both general settlements among airlines or bilateral agreements so as to define a set of rules for calculating flight tariffs.

The downstream process is split into three data outflows similar to the upstream process. The first data outflow sends invoice information to other airlines. The second data outflow transports accounting information to the parent company's ERP-system. The third data outflow provides financial information for the internal management information system.

FIGURE 3. The Business Model of the Company

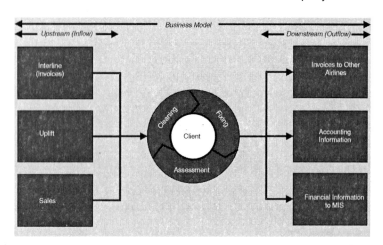

Concerning IT-infrastructure a proprietary application system supports the entire process model which has been designed and developed by the IT department of the company. Basically, the application system is due to the SAP R/3 workbench that serves as the software environment for all modules. This approach tries to combine the advantages of standard application packages and individual software solutions. On the one side the workbench provides access to widely accepted IT-standards like ABAP/4 as a 4GL-language for programming; on the other side the individual solution allows to develop process-centric applications that are not generally covered by application packages.

However, the company faces a delicate situation as business processes and IT environment are aligned insufficiently which inhibits effective prorating. Furthermore, existing knowledge management initiatives concentrate on technological or content aspects. Thus, knowledge management is grouped around questions like "which database technology fits best to our application landscape?" or "which information should be stored in our knowledge base?" More and more the company becomes aware that essentially a consistent knowledge management framework covering different characteristics beyond IT and questions of content is required. Although the framework should encompass a variety of aspects, the company requires a pragmatic approach as too academic methods has been deeply disappointing in the past. Additionally, there is an upcoming alertness for cultural aspects within the knowledge management subject. Employees are occasionally reluctant to share information, even thought technological and procedural requirements are fully provided. In sum, how to cope with all these aspects?

In order to address and answer key questions the company commences projects which are divided into several sub-projects. The most important sub-projects, that pursue the alignment of business processes and IT, stand outside the spotlight of this paper, because the focus lies on the knowledge management sub-project.

The entire project and therefore for knowledge management as well runs six months with a permanent engagement of four external consultants. However, the knowledge management sub-project merely requires a temporary commitment of both internal employees and external consultants of about one day per week. The sub-project pursues different objectives for knowledge management:

- To introduce not only a pragmatic, but also holistic framework within the project and later within the organization.
- To link business processes and knowledge management.
- To initiate and coach a permanent knowledge management group within the organization which is able to continue the process after the official project ends.

All results are regularly reported to the review board of the project by the knowledge management task force.

### Knowledge Management

The company has already started a lot of knowledge management activities in the past that have been uncoordinated to some extend and concentrated often on pure technological aspects. Thus, a reserved attitude towards new knowledge management activities is regarded especially concerning the relationship between the operating and the IT department.

The objectives for the knowledge management project are formulated based on the previous experiences:

- Definition of a conceptual framework for the design of the entire knowledge management project that is able to integrate and balance different departmental views.
- Theoretical and practical capability to apply the conceptual framework by the members of the knowledge management task force, so

that these members can continue the knowledge management process without external coaching.

- Practical application of the conceptual framework in terms of an exemplary business process as a "knowledge management showcase."
- Organizational implementation of the show case that should serve as a knowledge management nucleus for subsequent activities.

The task force decides to choose the knowledge supply chain matrix as a conceptual model for the entire knowledge management project. Moreover, out of all business processes within airline revenue accounting a special billing procedure in the interline stream is selected as an appropriate example for the show case. The interline stream is basically divided into two different types: non-sampling and sampling.

- Non-sampling is a generally accepted way to monetarily assess flight coupons based on negotiated agreements among airlines.
- Sampling in contrast is a simplified method to charge flight coupons based on a random sample.

The knowledge management task force focuses on the non-sampling procedure and starts with a high-level analysis. The analysis pursues to describe the sub-processes in the non-sampling procedure and to identify interesting knowledge content that may be served as input for the knowledge supply chain matrix.

In the non-sampling show case five sub-processes are recognized.

1. Sort in-box invoices according to different types.
2. Check sorted invoices based on international standards.
3. Enter invoice data into the IT system.
4. Technically re-check the data by system.
5. Manually judge the airlines concerning the financial liability.

The operating department sees in the last sub-process an ideal application for knowledge management as an employee has to judge over 1,000 airline companies for their credit liability in order to schedule unsecure receivables first. This ability requires a broad experience in airline billing that is frequently held as implicit knowledge by employees. The task force decides to choose this quality judgement of airlines as an appropriate knowledge asset to span the knowledge supply chain matrix.

In order to uncover implicit knowledge the task force interviews the non-sampling specialists. The first results show that quantitative as well as qualitative criteria describe the credit liability of airlines. Based on these criteria a rating model is developed for three types of airlines with a high, moderate or low credit liability (see Figure 4). The rating model represents the first field in the knowledge management matrix as it describes the content (factor strategy) for the knowledge generation. Additionally, not only detailed processes and responsible process owners for the knowledge generation (factor organization) has to be defined, but also the appropriate information technology (factor resource) must be provided. So, the aim is to complete all fields within the knowledge supply chain matrix that finally results in an operational concept as the summary of all functional requirements.

## CONCLUSION

The knowledge supply chain matrix is an appropriate tool to structure and balance knowledge management initiatives. Especially the underlying "fit"-idea promises to integrate a variety of different interests and viewpoints within knowledge management projects. Moreover, the knowledge supply chain matrix is simple enough to sell the basic ideas

FIGURE 4. The Quality Rating for Airlines in the Knowledge Supply Chain Matrix

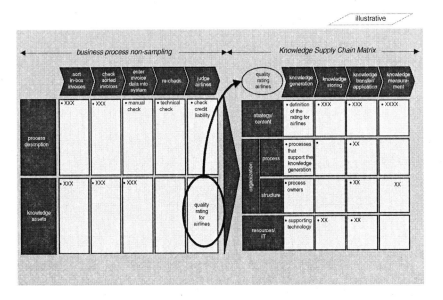

in front of different audiences as well as it is complex enough (at least to some extend) to answer the most important questions in the context of knowledge management. For this purpose the concept is successful.

However, the knowledge supply chain matrix follows a theoretical background that has caused some discussions. Especially within the knowledge management community, this type of process model caused some critical comments (Hilse, 2000: p. 218 f.; Willke, 1998, p. 78-79), because process models presume that knowledge can be managed in terms of analysis, implementation and controlling.

Basically, this knowledge supply chain matrix supports the functionalistic paradigm in contrast to the interpretative one. Burell and Morgan explained the differences between both standpoints. Concerning the functionalistic approach they write: "It is a perspective which is highly pragmatic in orientation, concerned to understand society in a way which generates knowledge which can be put to use. It is often problem-oriented in approach, concerned to provide practical solution to practical problems (Burell & Morgan, 1979: p. 26). And the interpretative paradigm: "The interpretative paradigm is informed by a concern to understand the world as it is, to understand the fundamental nature of the social world at the level of subjective experience. It seeks explanation within the realm of individual consciousness and subjectivity within the frame of the participant as opposed to the observer of action" (Burell & Morgan, 1979: p. 28).

Functionalistic approaches as the knowledge supply chain matrix hardly consider interpretative aspects. Therefore, beyond all technological or organizational problems that are addressed in knowledge management projects there is an spectrum of questions that is still not answered and that is still the source for disappointing initiatives-not only in knowledge management. A careful enhancement of functionalistic concepts with interpretative tools might promise a rewarding way to increase the probability for successful knowledge management projects.

## REFERENCES

Ansoff, I. (1979). *Strategic Management*. London.
Bea, F. X. B./Haas, J. (2001). *Strategisches Management*, Stuttgart.
Bergmann, K. (1999). die Bausteine des Wissensmanagements. In: Antoni, C.H./ Sommerlatte, T. (Hg.): *Report Wissensmanagement: Wie deutsche Firmen ihr Wissen profitabel machen*, Düsseldorf, 1999, 34-38.

Bock, F. (1998). The Intelligent Organization. In: Arthur D. Little: *Prism–Knowledge Management: Reaping the benefits*, 2, 5-15.

Burell, G./Morgan G. (1979). *Sociological Paradigm and Organizational Analysis.* London.

Chandler, A. D. (1962). *Strategy and Structure.* Cambridge.

Davenport, T.H./Prusak, L. (1998). *Working Knowledge: How Organizations Manage What They Know.* Boston.

Güldenberg, S. (1998). *Wissensmanagement und Wissenscontrolling in Lernenden Organisationen. Ein systemtheoretischer Ansatz*, Wiesbaden.

Hamel, G./Prahalad, C. (1990). The Core Competence of the Corporation. In: *Harvard Business Review*, May-June, 79-91.

Hamel, G./Prahalad, C. (1994). *Competing for the Future.* Boston.

Hattendorf, M. (2002). Wissensmanagement–Problemprozesse und Problem Prozesse. In: Mohe, M./Heinecke, H. J./Pfriem, R. *Consulting–Problemlösung als Geschäftsmodell. Theorie, Praxis, Markt*, 180-194.

Hilse, H. (2000). *Kognitive Wende in Management und Beratung: Wissensmanagement aus Sozialwissenschaftlicher Perspektive.* Wiesbaden.

Little, Arthur D. (1991). (Ed.). *Management der Hochleistungsorganisation.* Wiesbaden.

Little, Arthur D. (1995). (Ed.). *Management der Lernprozesse im Unternehmen.* Wiesbaden.

Little, Arthur D. (1999). *Knowledge management–managing intellectual assets for value creation*, company brochure about knowledge management.

Mandl, H. (2001). *Wissensmanagement lernen.* Vortrag auf der Konferenz Professionelles Wissensmanagement–Erfahrungen und Visionen, Baden-Baden.

Mandl, H./Reinmann-Rothmeier, G. (2000). Die Rolle des Wissensmanagements für die Zukunft. In: Mandl, H./Reinmann-Rothmeier, G.: *Wissensmanagement.* München, 1-17.

Porter, M. E. (1980). *Competitive Strategy.* New York.

Porter, M. E. (1985). *Competitive Advantage.* New York.

Waterman, R. Jr./Peters, T. J. (1982). *In Search of Excellence.* New York.

Waterman, R. Jr./Peters, T. J./Phillips, J.R. (1980). Structure Is Not Organization. In: *Business Horizons*, 23, 3, 14-26.

Willke, H. (1998). *Systemisches Wissensmanagement.* Stuttgart.

# The Knowledge Café–
# A Knowledge Management System
# and Its Application
# to Hospitality and Tourism

Norbert Gronau

**SUMMARY.** Knowledge management is identified as a key success factor in most industries today. While data or information can be stored independently from people, knowledge is bound to people who use it for their interactions. The main goal of knowledge management is to improve the usage of knowledge in the enterprise. Knowledge management systems are not only organizational memory information systems. They also contain organizational standard procedures and a certain cultural attitude. A reference framework gives implementation hints mainly influenced by technical possibilities. The knowledge management system reference architecture contains layers of sources, repositories, taxonomy, services, applications and user interfaces. A software tool that largely corresponds to this reference framework is the Knowledge Café. Possible applications of this tool to the area of hospitality and tourism are described in this paper. *[Article copies available for a fee from The Haworth Document Delivery Service: 1-800-HAWORTH. E-mail address: <docdelivery@*

Norbert Gronau is Professor of Business Information Systems, University of Oldenburg, Department of Computer Science, Escherweg 2, 26212 Oldenburg, Germany (E-Mail: gronau@informatik.uni-oldenburg.de).

[Haworth co-indexing entry note]: "The Knowledge Café–A Knowledge Management System and Its Application to Hospitality and Tourism." Gronau, Norbert. Co-published simultaneously in *Journal of Quality Assurance in Hospitality & Tourism* (The Haworth Hospitality Press, an imprint of The Haworth Press, Inc.) Vol. 3, No. 3/4, 2002, pp. 75-88; and: *Knowledge Management in Hospitality and Tourism* (ed: Ricarda B. Bouncken and Sungsoo Pyo) The Haworth Hospitality Press, an imprint of The Haworth Press, Inc., 2002, pp. 75-88. Single or multiple copies of this article are available for a fee from The Haworth Document Delivery Service [1-800-HAWORTH, 9:00 a.m. - 5:00 p.m. (EST). E-mail address: docdelivery@haworthpress.com].

10.1300/J162v03n03_05

**KEYWORDS.** Knowledge management, discovery, collaboration

## KNOWLEDGE MANAGEMENT

Knowledge can be defined as the sum of information and capabilities that individuals use in arriving at solutions to problems. Thus it can entail theoretical findings, practical every day rules or instructions for action. The availability of data and information is a prerequisite for knowledge. In contrast to this, however, knowledge is always tied to some type of interaction by people (Probst, 1998).

Knowledge management is defined as an operational management task that encompasses a decision-oriented approach. It is the goal of this management task to establish learning processes across all levels of the organization and to develop them consistently. An organizational knowledge base is one possible result of knowledge management in an entrepreneurial context (Davenport, 1998).

Since the knowledge of an organization exists in an unstructured and dynamic form, the use of information technology should have the purpose of rediscovering internal and external data and methods and referring them to human experts. Support systems for this application can be called OMIS (Organizational Memory Information Systems), competency or know-how databases (Ackerman, 1994).

### Components of a Knowledge Management System

In the following section, the necessary components for a knowledge management system–from the viewpoint of the authors–will be discussed.

The goal of knowledge management is to improve organizational capabilities and the efficiency of the implementation of the organizational strategy while consistently using knowledge as a resource. The basic approach of knowledge management is to capture documents, personal experience and all other categories of information and to provide it in a manner that is useful to reach the goals of the organization (Lawton, 2001: 11). An important task in this context is to analyze the demand of knowledge that is needed by the members of the organization to support the reaching of the goals of the organization in the best possible way.

Additionally internal and external sources of knowledge are to identify which can satisfy the knowledge demand concerning process knowledge, knowledge of the members of the organization or of stakeholders. Knowledge that is not available in an explicit form, e.g., in documents, databases, formulas or technical data should be explicated. Experience, capabilities, unwritten rules (also named as tacit or quiet knowledge) should be converted in a digital form (this is called externalization) (Nonaka, 1994: 14) or transferred to other members of the organization (socialization). So it is possible for the organization to access and share its knowledge. The so gained and externalized knowledge needs to be structured, presented, cultivated and administrated.

Knowledge management systems (KMS) support the channeling of existing sources of knowledge. An additional goal of a knowledge management system is to provide relevant information at any time and anywhere to help members of the organization to solve problems related to their tasks.

Therefore different sources of knowledge have to be integrated. The categorization and classification of knowledge should be possible automatically or manually. KMS deliver tools for easy input of information in different ways like adding new information by members of the organization, automatic inspection of electronic documents like e-mail or by indexation of external contents (data bases, CD-ROM). Prerequisites for the keeping of this kind of knowledge are the definition of knowledge goals, the creation of a uniform organizational structure and a company culture which stimulates the exchange of information and knowledge. Information technology has to map structures and processes of the organization. The biggest amount of collected information is only useful if transparency and ease of use are available. Therefore, extensive information retrieval functions and knowledge distribution mechanisms are necessary.

The characteristics of a knowledge management system separated from other business information systems can be described using an architecture that is divided into six layers (Figure 1).

*Information and knowledge sources*, which in light of the increasing digitalization of contents make up the overwhelming portion of the available information in organizations, are dedicated to be the basis of the knowledge management system. In hospitality and tourism possible knowledge sources can be the contents of files on a server, intranet pages, directory of business relevant persons, e-mail traffic that is guided

FIGURE 1. Architecture of a Knowledge Management System

| Interfaces | Knowledge Portal | | | |
|---|---|---|---|---|
| Applications | Collaborative Applications | E-Learning Applications | ... | |
| Services | Collaboration Services | Discovery Services | Publishing Services | Template Services |
| Taxonomy | Taxonomy | | | |
| Information Management | Knowledge Repositories — Template Structure (meta data)   Content   User Rights Management | | | |
| Sources | texts in file system | Internet/ intranet | directory of persons   e-mail   databases   document archives   audio-visual media files   ... | | |

to specialists for certain situations (e.g., for technical maintenance). Additional potential sources of knowledge are databases that probably contain reports and relevant data for business cases. If a document management system is available this is a potential knowledge source, too. In the near future it will be possible to analyze and segment audio and video files so that they can be used in KMS in circumstances other than what they were created for.

A *knowledge repository* integrates the different sources and ensures a uniform, logical view of the variety of sources. This is a condition for the processing of knowledge sources by the higher levels of the system architecture.

A structured presentation of the knowledge available in the system that can be used for navigation is made available by the *taxonomy* layer. Some existing implementations also integrate knowledge repository and taxonomy into a single component. Glossaries, key word lists and thesauri are used to form a taxonomy. This is a useful component especially in the field of tourism and hospitality where employees have a higher turnover rate than in other industries. The use of taxonomy makes it easier to understand the special terms in this industry.

The service layer provides some service components based on the lower layers and is used by the application layer. The differentiation in services and application layers is an architectural decision which points out the possibility to distribute services in a network environment and which separates applications (with a user defined goal) from services (with a system defined function). At least four services are necessary to be able to create knowledge management applications:

- A primary function is *search*, which is provided by the discovery services. A differentiation between pull and push technologies (other sources refer to this as active and passive techniques) can be made. In a *pull situation* (or with an active search) the user searches the knowledge management system by inputting a search string. The stimulus for generating the knowledge thus comes from the user. In a *push situation* (or a passive search) based on a customized interest profile, the user receives unsolicited and automatically generated documents that have been newly added to the knowledge management system based on his/her interest profile with every usage of the system. The advantage of the push technology is that no stimulus from the user is needed to generate the output of knowledge. With skillful utilization of the interest profile, other relevant documents are also found, which would not have been retrieved using the traditional pull technology.
- *Collaboration services* allow a distributed cooperation between different persons at different times. Examples for collaborative services are workflows for document approval or the work on texts or graphical models by a group whose members are located at different sites.
- *Publication services* deliver functionality to publish a document in the intranet.
- *Template services* allow creation and administration of templates for the storage of different kind of information in different document types.

The functionality of a knowledge management system on the *application* layer is constructed using the services of the service layer. Some examples for knowledge management applications in hospitality and tourism are described at the end of this paper.

The *user interface* layer provides a uniform interface for the operation of the system, which may be customizable. Personal customization is an important requirement for the success of knowledge management systems because different user types exist. A differentiation of user types is possible regarding the user's experience (inexperienced, well-informed, expert) Additionally, the demand for information the user needs is important for a typology. Every employee belongs to a certain department and works in certain processes. He will be interested at first in information about his department and processes and then about others if this information is easily accessible for him. Customization allows the creation of favorite links, a personal start page with extended information on his department and processes and introductory information on others. The discovery services will help the user to find out more if necessary.

## THE KNOWLEDGE CAFÉ–
## A TYPICAL KNOWLEDGE MANAGEMENT SYSTEM

The Knowledge Café, developed in 1999 by Berlin University of Technology (Krallmann, 2000: 205; Gronau, 2001: 77) and now distributed by altavier (altavier, 2002), is a modular knowledge management system based on the above-discussed architectural framework. It contains a basic module with glossary, newsletter, full text search and help and can integrate different components like yellow pages, knowledge base, virtual library, discussion and project module.

The Knowledge Café can be used either with a browser or with Lotus Notes client software. The access to the contents of the modules is realized by hyperlink structures and with user-friendly context-sensitive full text search engines. All documents in the system are characterized by keywords from the glossary. Figure 2 shows the architecture of the Knowledge Café.

### Yellow Pages

The access of existing knowledge in the enterprise is often difficult because corresponding competencies of employees are known only inside the borders of work groups and departments (Choo, 1998; Tunik, 2001).

Yellow pages are helpful if the right contact partners are searched or a project team has to be assembled which should correspond with the requirements of the problem to be solved.

Employees can be found corresponding to their qualification, experience and competency. Persons also can be found under criteria like position in the organization (location, branch offices, departments, etc.), project participation and name.

The basis for these functions is a personal home page for each employee (cf. Figure 3). In this document actual and past work areas, project

FIGURE 2. Architecture of the Knowledge Café

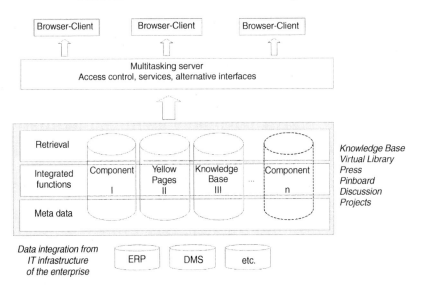

FIGURE 3. Personal Homepage in the Yellow Pages Module of the Knowledge Café

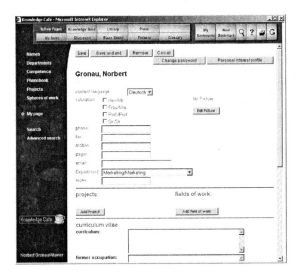

experience and competencies are stored. Every employee can take care of his own personal home page because the entry and publication of information in an intranet is very easy with the Knowledge Café.

## Knowledge Base–Topic Centered Pool of Information

Employees collect experience, create reports and contribute with their work to the success of the enterprise. The intranet can be very helpful to facilitate the access to experience, opinions and documents of relevant topics for many employees. Figure 4 shows the creation of a new entry in the knowledge base.

With this module knowledge can be provided either for all employees or for special interest groups. So knowledge which was not known till now will be distributed and can be used extensively. Double working is reduced and the experience of other people helps to process tasks faster and in better quality.

The knowledge base supports the generation, use and distribution of competencies in an enterprise. It forms the technological basis for a topic-oriented discussion.

The publication of documents and the access of different contents is controlled by an access control system. So it will be possible to give

FIGURE 4. Creation of a New Entry in the Knowledge Base

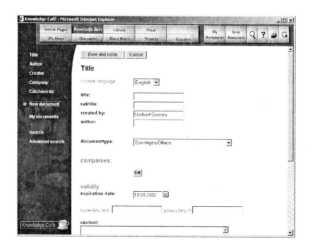

only the members of a project group access to their documents. All documents are categorized based on the entries of the glossary. Documents in other file formats can be embedded easily (e.g., Lotus Smart Suite, Acrobat PDF files, MS Word, etc.).

## *Virtual Library–Management and Publication of Documents in the Intranet*

Although lots of documents exist in enterprises, employees often have neither knowledge of the existence of these documents nor access to these books, journals, papers and other relevant publications. In the virtual library employees can search efficiently for documents and read them either in a digital form or be informed about the source location. Contrary to the knowledge base only a few responsible persons with the role "librarian" publish documents in the virtual library that can be accessed by either all employees or specified groups. The basis for access is an access control system that prevents unauthorized access to certain documents. The duration of a publication period in the intranet can be chosen so that after a certain period of time the document disappears and will be archived. An archived document will be found using the discovery services but is not seen in document catalogs sorted by key words. An example for the creation of a new document in the virtual library is shown in Figure 5.

FIGURE 5. Creation of a New Virtual Library Entry

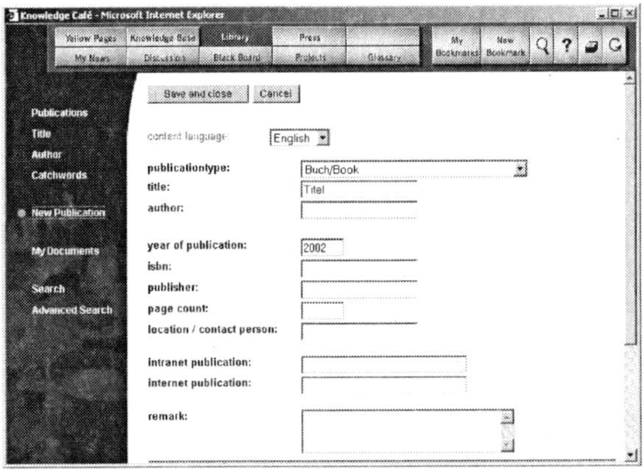

### Discussion Groups–Expert Circles in the Intranet

Using this module, employees can discuss self-chosen topics. Topics, discussion contributions and responses to these contributions can be stored in this module up to a depth of 17 levels. With this module it is possible to form expert circles. Other employees who have questions about certain topics will also benefit from these discussions.

The generation of a dynamic discussion culture can be controlled and supported actively by the enterprise. Electronic discussion groups are useful in hospitality and tourism to give inexperienced employees hints for their tasks. Online discussions allow participants from different locations to join. This is a great advantage particularly in the international industry of hospitality and tourism. Additionally, it is possible to store intermediate results from a discussion for some months until other participants are able to continue the topic.

### Project Module–Knowledge-Based Project Management

The module is separated into a public and an internal project area. In the public area the projects are commonly described and selected documents are published for (nearly) all employees. In the internal area where only project members have access the project is organized, all project-related documents are stored, people, dates and resources of the project are administrated and the communication within the project is supported.

Advantages of the project module are the publication of project results and solution alternatives in the intranet. Therefore, employees with similar problems in other projects can use existing experience. Additionally, it is easier to find colleagues who are familiar with certain problems and their solutions.

## APPLICATION OF KNOWLEDGE MANAGEMENT SYSTEMS IN THE AREA OF HOSPITALITY AND TOURISM

Possible application areas of knowledge management systems in hospitality and tourism are business planning, service operations, quality improvement and reaction on emergency cases. For each of these application areas a configuration example of the Knowledge Café is described.

Every scenario is based on a common glossary that contains the relevant vocabulary in this industry, synonyms and an explanation of each term.

## Business Planning

Business planning involves the process of planning capacities, quality standards and prices of airplanes, hotels and additional services. This is a collaborative task with participants in different roles like seller, buyer and middlemen. To make the business planning process easier it is useful to store relevant information about different people and their roles in the process in the yellow page module, so it is possible to find out who has experience in certain countries or with foreign government procedures. As the number of participants in the business planning process increases, it becomes more difficult to find the person able to answer one's questions.

The virtual library is a possible storage location for standard operating procedures, e.g., for calculation of prices, capacities and reports. Documents in the library are accessible for every authorized user of the system.

## Service Operations

Applications in service operations are between hotel facilities planning, event scheduling or the creation of restaurant menu selections. Information about vineyards, hotel characteristics or cooking constraints can be stored and classified in the virtual library. Actual work in progress can be accompanied either by the knowledge base or by the project module. The news flash function of the Knowledge Café keeps people informed without an inquiry being made. An example from hospitality may explain this function. A food procurement manager is interested in the region of California, in vineyards and in poultry. He chooses these keywords from the glossary of the Knowledge Café and stores them into his personal interest profile. Now a hotel manager from the same company enters a new suggestion of menu selection containing Californian Chardonnay (white wine) into the knowledge base. He classifies this new document with some keywords from the glossary, too.

The next time the procurement manager enters the system and checks his "MyNews" area, he will be informed about the new document that was entered by the hotel manager. Now the procurement manager can generate the knowledge that in future more Chardonnay will be needed and that it would be a good idea to look for some sources with high quality.

### Quality Improvement

The process of quality improvement can be settled up on the same system that is used for business planning. For managing customer complaints the integration of web-based forms is necessary. Paper-based quality questionnaires can be entered into the system either by automatic character recognition or by helpers. Using the project module of the Knowledge Café, the definition of workflows based on customer complaints, the investigation of their causes and their remedy are possible. Experience won in these processes can be used for future business planning processes.

### Reaction on Emergency Cases

In emergency cases an extremely fast reaction on operative, administrative and strategic level is necessary. Standard procedures stored in the virtual library of the Knowledge Café help to do the right things even in crisis situations. If plans of hotels, airports and streets are stored in the virtual library, the Knowledge Café should be accessible also for external participants.

## CONCLUSION AND FURTHER DEVELOPMENT

Knowledge management systems are a combination of different services basing on several sources connected with the system by a repository layer. A realization of the knowledge management framework architecture is the Knowledge Café. Some examples from the area of hospitality and tourism show that there is a broad range of use possibilities for knowledge management systems.

To reach a return on investment after the installation of a knowledge management system (Harvard, 2001), it is necessary to integrate knowledge management functions in existing intranets (Logan, 2001; Gronau/ Kalisch, 2002).

Actually the Knowledge Café is an "all-in-one" system with components adjusted to work fine with another. Problems can occur if a third party search engine like case based reasoning (Aha, 1999; Gronau/ Laskowski, 2002) or an automatic text classification program should interact with the Knowledge Café. Therefore one development task will be the partitioning of the system in smaller components which can be used in heterogeneous software environments (Saha, 2001) and together with other knowledge management tools.

The other development task is the evolution from a company specific knowledge management tool to a knowledge community tool. The most important step on this way is the proper integration of customers and their representatives (e.g., travel agencies) and to open the possibility of discussion with customers and to learn from their experience without surrendering proprietary business information.

## REFERENCES

Ackerman, M.S. (1994). *Answer Garden: A Tool for Growing Organizational Memory*. MIT Sloan School of Management (PhD Thesis). Boston.

Aha, D.W.; Muñoz-Avila, H. (1999). *Exploring Synergies of Knowledge Management and Case-Based Reasoning*: Papers from the AAAI 1999 Workshop. Washington, DC: Naval Research Laboratory, Navy Center for Applied Research in Artificial Intelligence.

altavier (2002). *Company home page.* http://www.altavier.de (last accessed May 14, 2002).

Choo, C. (1998). *The Knowing Organization–How Organizations Use Information to Construct Meaning, Create Knowledge, and Make Decisions.* Oxford University Press.

Davenport, T., Prusak, L. (1998). *Working Knowledge. How Organizations Manage What They Know.* Harvard Business School Press.

Gronau, N., Schönherr, M. (2001). Introduction of the Knowledge Management System Knowledge Café into a tax consultancy company. In: Bauknecht, K., Brauer, W., Mück, Th. (Hrsg.): *Informatik 2001. Business and Science in the Network Economy–Visions and Reality.* Vienna, p. 77-83 (in German).

Gronau, N., Laskowski, F. (2002). *Integrating CBR Functionality into a KM System: The TO_KNOW Approach.* Accepted Paper. Proc. of the 2002 International Conference on Information and Knowledge Engineering, Las Vegas (NV).

Gronau, N., Kalisch, A. (2002). *Knowledge Content Management System–A Framework integrating Content Management and Knowledge Management.* Accepted Paper. Proc. of the 2002 International Conference on Information and Knowledge Engineering, Las Vegas (NV).

Harvard Computing Group (2001). *Report: Knowledge Management–Return on Investment. http://www.kmadvantage.com/docs/KM/KM_-_ROI.pdf,* (last accessed Nov. 15 2001).

Krallmann, H. et al. (2000). Knowledge Management in the Category Consulting Department of a Service Company. In: Krallmann, H., Gronau, N.: *Competitive Ad-*

*vantages Through Knowledge Management.* Stuttgart: Schaeffer-Poeschel, p. 205-238 (in German).

Lawton, G. (2001). Knowledge Management: Ready for Prime Time? *Computer* 1, p 11-13.

Logan, D. (2001). *Content Management Needs Knowledge Management.* In: Gartner Group Research Note from Feb. 23 2001.

Nonaka, I. (1994). A dynamic theory of organizational knowledge creation. *Organization Science* 5, p. 14-37.

Probst, G. Raub, S., Romhardt, K. (1999). *Manage the Knowledge. How companies optimally use their most valuable resource* (in German). 3rd Edition. Frankfurt (Main): FAZ-Verlag.

Saha, A. (2002). *Application Framework for e-business: Portals. http://www-106. ibm.com/developerworks/library/portals/* (last accessed Feb. 10, 2002).

Tunik Morello, D. (2001). *Leading Motivating and Supporting the Workforce of the New Knowledge Economy.* In: Gartner Group Strategic Analysis Report from Sept. 24 2001.

# Cross-Border Destination Management Systems in the Alpine Region– The Role of Knowledge Networks on the Example of AlpNet

Harald Pechlaner
Dagmar Abfalter
Frieda Raich

**SUMMARY.** The Alps are the focus of a wide-ranging discussion. Researchers, scientists, politicians, inhabitants, and people who earn their living in the Alpine region are all confronted with difficult challenges. The main topics are the development in the fields of nature, landscape, tourism and leisure, traffic and transport, and its consequences for the Alps as a living space and economic area. About 30 years ago, a cooperation of tourism and political authorities in 11 countries, regions, provinces, and cantons of Switzerland, Germany, Italy, and Austria has been established. Due to globalization and changing traveling patterns, people

---

Harald Pechlaner and Dagmar Abfalter are affiliated with the University of Innsbruck, Department of General and Tourism Management, Universitäts-Str. 15, A-6020 Innsbruck, Austria.

Frieda Raich is affiliated with Eurac Research, Department of Tourism Management, Drusus-Str. 1, I-39100 Bozen, Italy.

[Haworth co-indexing entry note]: "Cross-Border Destination Management Systems in the Alpine Region–The Role of Knowledge Networks on the Example of AlpNet." Pechlaner, Harald, Dagmar Abfalter, and Frieda Raich. Co-published simultaneously in *Journal of Quality Assurance in Hospitality & Tourism* (The Haworth Hospitality Press, an imprint of The Haworth Press, Inc.) Vol. 3, No. 3/4, 2002, pp. 89-107; and: *Knowledge Management in Hospitality and Tourism* (ed: Ricarda B. Bouncken and Sungsoo Pyo) The Haworth Hospitality Press, an imprint of The Haworth Press, Inc., 2002, pp. 89-107. Single or multiple copies of this article are available for a fee from The Haworth Document Delivery Service [1-800-HAWORTH, 9:00 a.m. - 5:00 p.m. (EST). E-mail address: docdelivery@haworthpress.com].

10.1300/J162v03n03_06

have become more and more aware that a new international cooperation of the Alpine tourism regions in the field of destination management and marketing is required. This is necessary in order to react to market changes accordingly. This acknowledgment is instead of small and more or less independent and self-sufficient organizations. It also includes the collaboration concerning one of the most important resources of our time–knowledge–and the establishment of a network where it can be consciously managed.

The following paper shows the special qualities of networks, especially knowledge networks at the example of AlpNet. It consists of three parts. The first part deals with the change of Alpine tourism management and marketing, the second part discusses the necessities and challenges of a cross-border cooperation in tourism marketing with a special focus on networks and knowledge networks, and the third part presents the results of an empirical study explaining the problems and perspectives for developing knowledge networks of cross-border destination management in the Alpine region. As far as management and marketing of tourism destinations are concerned, it is shown what possibilities–yet what limits–may result in launching cross-border cooperation projects in the future. For decades cross-border cooperation was used for compensating existing competitive disadvantages on tourism markets. The example of the new project AlpNet shows how important cooperation and member-specific requirements are for tourism and other economic industries when it comes to the establishment of knowledge networks. *[Article copies available for a fee from The Haworth Document Delivery Service: 1-800-HAWORTH. E-mail address: <docdelivery@haworthpress.com> Website: <http://www.HaworthPress. com> © 2002 by The Haworth Press, Inc. All rights reserved.]*

**KEYWORDS.** Alpine tourism, destination management and marketing, networks, knowledge management and networks, cross-border cooperation

## THE CHANGE OF ALPINE TOURISM MANAGEMENT AND MARKETING

Providing a segment-specific service bundle in a certain destination could become a difficult task. A great number of combined tourism service bundles would have to be provided due to the increasing individualization of guest segments (see, e.g., Gartner & Lime, 2000), as well as social circumstances in traditional tourism destinations. This means that central control would become impossible. Traditional destinations of the Alpine area have continuously grown and lead to a broad dispersal of property. This development shows a coordination problem that may not be solved by central authorities. Public goods and the decentralized innovation potential of tourism entrepreneurs are further reasons for difficulties of a central management and organization authority (Pechlaner & Tschurtschenthaler, 2002). Cooperative relationships can guarantee vital tasks and functions of destination management through a high number of service carriers involved. They internalize positive external effects. The more cooperation within a region, the higher the competitiveness of the region (Smeral, 1998). Numerous authors point out at the importance of a centralized coordinating body for the tourism of a destination (for an overview see Bieger, 2002, 69 pp.). Tourism organizations fulfill those tasks and functions of tourism destinations that may be carried out in a cross-border and cooperative way. This includes the planning, strategy and development function (see, e.g., Inskeep, 1991, 411), and the coordination function of a tourism destination or region essential for providing tourism activities and the marketing function.

General cooperation requirements have not changed; their intensity has changed. Demand is decreasing for tourism services, particularly in traditional destinations of the Alpine region. Rigidity of organizational structures, increasing dependency of distribution partners, consumption of entrepreneurial substance at small and medium-sized businesses, as well as competitiveness of the whole sector in traditional tourism countries are, together with the changes mentioned above, responsible for the crisis of tourism organizations in Alpine destinations (Pechlaner & Sauerwein, 2002).

The most important limits of cooperative marketing and management of traditional destinations of the Alpine region may be summarized as follows (Pechlaner & Tschurtschenthaler, 2002):

- Insufficient investment in projects and innovation lead to a small number of clearly defined concepts;
- provider heterogeneity;
- political abundance and minor use of resources in tourism organizations make it impossible to clearly position destinations;
- the benefit deficit of tourism organizations perceived by its members leads to a high pressure to react, this again results in an extension of the tasks within a tourism organization, yet has only in

some cases really improved effectiveness and efficiency of the tourism organization;

- little optimized service chains result in unsatisfied guests as gaps between the single services of a destination sometimes have negative impact on the quality assessment of the visitor;
- product bundles need a high capability and willingness to cooperate, the high share of public financing (through direct investment, rates, and taxes) often requires a certain neutrality of tourism organizations toward its members leading to expensive arrangements;
- according to tourism organizations, innovation is a public good, it is not their task to create innovative products, but to provide an innovative climate;
- the fragmentation of tourism service providers largely impedes the access to relevant markets, therefore market research studies carried out by the tourism organizations or commissioned to an institute are mostly regarded as a public good; and
- from a holistic point of view, tourism organizations are more inner-oriented than outer-oriented.

## CROSS-BORDER COOPERATION– THE ROLE OF KNOWLEDGE NETWORKS

Even though the Alpine region tourism is confronted with a high number of changing parameters and a high parameter changing speed within the environment, these trends still exist (compare, e.g., Gartner & Lime, 2000; Keller, 1996):

1. Deregulation tendencies of national economies;
2. development in the field of information and communication technologies;
3. internationalization and globalization of supply and demand parameters;
4. network economies accelerate the formation of cooperation networks of different industries (Laesser & Jaeger, 2001), and
5. changed expectations and increasing disloyalty of the consumer.

These trends make it necessary to form cooperations in an economic context characterized by small- and medium-sized structures, such as the Alpine region. These structures make it difficult for service providers in the Alpine region to realize the economies of scope. Cooperations are a chance for small- and medium-sized organizations to improve their own market position (together with cooperation partners), without losing their independence. Cooperations lead to positive effects, as product attractiveness of cooperating companies may only be guaranteed by a network of relation exchanges. The integration of small- and medium- sized companies among the local and regional networks is again the basis for new networks on a transregional level. Increasing cost pressure, rationalization, and allocation difficulties are additional reasons for reviewing a traditional organization policy focusing on persisting alone in predatory competition. The regional integration of economic areas (e.g., European Union) boosts efforts for international cooperation.

### Networks: An Approach for Cross-Border Cooperation

In the framework of current trends in cooperation management, networks are leading toward a new direction of the discussion. Networks (of companies) are polycentric systems. According to Sydow (1992, 79) a business network is an organizational form of economic activities aiming at achieving competitive advantages. It is characterized by complex, reciprocal, rather cooperative than competitive, and relatively stable relationships between legally independent, yet economically dependent companies. This interpretation unifies elements of market, hierarchy, cooperation, and competitiveness. In doing so, this settles the conflict between the dichotomy of market and hierarchy. The definition of network used in the following paragraph is seen from an inter-organizational network perspective (Riggers, 1998). It is not limited to a single corporation or network partner, but comprises network partners and their relationships to each other on a higher level.

Typically, networks show the following characteristics (Miles/Snow, 1986, 64):

- *Vertical disaggregation:* Various organizations within the network system take over tasks and functions of organizations defined as value creating activities along the value chain. For example, not every organization within a network fulfills all tasks, but concentrates on those tasks and functions where it has a core competence. Other tasks and functions are left to other network partners or are out-sourced.
- *Broker:* Network activities must be bundled by a broker in order to be able to design market relationships.

- *Market mechanisms:* They are responsible for a competition-oriented nature of network relations. Within a network both cooperation and competition exist at a similar amount. Competition within business networks is made possible due to redundancy, i.e., that sometimes the same activities are carried out by different network partners. This redundancy is responsible for security (despite dependency), flexibility (despite stability), competition (despite cooperation), and learning and innovation. Knowledge and innovation can only emerge from competition among a network system.
- *New information and communication systems:* They are responsible for improved communication between network members and sometimes they are even prerequisites. Information and communication systems ease the building of confidence within networks as bigger amounts of information are made accessible for all network members within a shorter period of time. Generally, confidence is the basis for the success of network systems (Parkhe, 1991; Niederkofler, 1991).

Strategic networks are a special form of networks. The term "strategic network" traces back to Jarillo (1988). Strategic networks are based on long-term and stable relational patterns (Miles & Snow, 1995). While strategic alliances usually concentrate on selected areas such as Research and Development and do not include a joint market appearance, strategic networks focus on a more efficient handling of operational cooperation with special respect to sales and marketing (Riggers, 1998). The strategy aspect is based on the joint goal of the network partners to enhance the competitive position of the network (Håkansson & Sharma, 1996). In literature, strategic alliances are treated from different points of views. The main focus is put on the generation of capabilities and knowledge (Hamel, 1991), competition (Burgers et al., 1993), and the procedural character of networks (Thomas & Trevino, 1993).

Essential to this concept of strategic networks is that of hub firm, which is the firm that sets up the network and takes a pro-active attitude in the care of it (Jarillo, 1988, 32). Depending on the design of a strategic network, partners can be involved in strategy decisions. The network partners try to generate a preferably large offer and guarantee efficient processes through an individual concentration on singular competencies. In many cases this is associated with a mutual use of resources such as knowledge. The management of strategic networks puts its main focus on the relationship between network members. These relationships may be characterized as follows (Campbell & Wilson, 1996, 139):

- *Willingness to invest:* The willingness of network members, for example, to invest and increase the value of the whole network in order to strengthen their own position. Apart from the agreements concluded with the network, investment also concentrates on creating joint values for a competition-oriented cooperation within the network. The more a network partner is able to create these values and, in doing so, granting stability to the network, the more intense the position of the partner is within the system.
- *Partner asymmetries:* Strategic networks have a hierarchical element strengthening their competitiveness. These hierarchies are based on contributions made by each network partner. The more a network partner contributes to enhance the value of the whole network, the more important his position is within the system. The position of a partner within a relationship bundle may be put on a level with the role of the partner compared to other partners with whom he is directly or indirectly linked. Partner asymmetries make hierarchies necessary in order to manage and/or control network resources.
- *Confidence:* This characteristic is a necessary resource in networks and allows for decreases in negotiation costs arising among cooperations. As long as network partners believe that they achieve advantages thanks to their network participation, they will support the joint goals and aims of the network (Jarillo, 1993).

### *Cross-Border Knowledge Networks of Tourism Destinations*

Decisive for the success of an organization is knowledge relevant for decisions, as well as current and well-processed knowledge. This is the only way to formulate strategies in time and to actively influence the turbulent environment (Nonaka & Takeuchi, 1995). This is the reason why knowledge may not be left to chance, but must be managed. Knowledge management goes into the question of what kind of knowledge activities such as knowledge generation, knowledge use, or knowledge transfer are inherent in organizations and should consciously be managed (von Krogh et al., 2000). The process of knowledge generation is of particular importance and may be compared with a spiral: The number of organizations, persons, and groups participating in the knowledge process and that their mutual interaction lead to an increase in knowledge (Nonaka & Takeuchi, 1995). Therefore, knowledge development must include as many people concerned as possible–the more persons and organizations are involved, the bigger the knowledge spiral (Malhotra, 2000). This is coherent with the finding that knowledge development in tourism regions depends on size (Bieger, 1998). Small tourism organizations may not generate all the information necessary and may not be able to process and interpret all of the information gathered. Therefore, a small tourism organization responsible for a limited area within the destination is not able to deduce trends and tendencies from limited information (Pechlaner & Tschurtschenthaler, 2002). There is a risk that they may lag behind developments, provide less innovative products, or create a distorted view of the situation. Forms of cooperation must be found, weighed up, and realized in order to overcome such a phenomena and weaknesses (Grant & Baden-Fuller, 2000).

For considering knowledge generation depending on size, for using the resource "knowledge" accordingly, destination organizations must create a network and exchange their knowledge among each other. This leads to a non-distorted view and to the collection of profound information material that may then be processed. Moreover, networks make it possible to provide comprehensive services for visitors (Håkansson & Ford, 2002). Cooperations are not only essential within a tourism destination, but also within other tourism destinations and their tourism organizations (Augustyn & Knowles, 2000). Networks should not be narrowed by seemingly rigid limits and regions determined by tourism policies, but should be cross-border systems. The visitor, due to increasing globalization, has a different perception of regions and is looking for spacious areas providing a wide range of experiences and activities. The aim is to overcome parish-pump politics, to recognize the whole region without distortions and to fulfill the needs and wishes of the tourist. Such cross-border knowledge networks enable intense knowledge generation in the following fields.

*Local knowledge development in the respective destinations:* Each destination may and should identify and generate local knowledge that may later be put together, analyzed, and completed.

*Cross-border knowledge development*: For example, overall knowledge of the region of all destinations concerned. This kind of knowledge is essential for the sustainable development of cross-border living spaces and tourism regions like the Alps. Generating knowledge means intense cooperation with other industries and heavy investment. Local and cross-border knowledge are interconnected, this means they influence each other.

*Meta knowledge*: For example, knowing what you know or being aware of knowledge allocation, strengths and weaknesses of local and regional knowledge pools, transparency of knowledge carriers, and awareness of interesting connections among different knowledge carriers. This kind of knowledge has strategic importance as it is the starting point for further knowledge activities.

Thanks to the interrelation of local, cross-border, and meta knowledge a cross-border knowledge spiral comes up, integrating diversified and supplementary knowledge due to partners from fields other than tourism (non-tourism members). This results in knowledge influencing the provision of activities, the overall network strategy, further destination strategies, and, in doing so, destination knowledge again.

Altogether, a knowledge network helps (Skyrme, 1999):

- To flexibly react to market requirements: Selective and cross-border gathering of information and generation of knowledge gives insights to development tendencies and enables an innovative provision of activities in time;
- to develop new core competencies: Knowledge is combined with other resources in order to be beneficial to the client and to create competitive advantages;
- to act despite limited resources without losing one's independence;
- to avoid undesirable trends: Broader and deeper knowledge supports the assessment of market developments;
- to achieve more customer satisfaction: Destinations know more about their guests, their wishes, and their behavior patterns and may therefore provide a comprehensive product; and
- to make use of synergies.

Prerequisites for successful knowledge networks are forcing the process of knowledge generation and sharing as well as gaining confidence (Seufert et al., 1999). Each destination is integrated into various formal and informal networks and must therefore manage a portfolio of alliances (Wilkinson & Young, 2002). Relationships established by a destination should contribute to knowledge and resources which complete their knowledge and existing resources. Streams of knowledge must be thoroughly built up and cultivated. Again and again phenomena impeding an adequate and cross-border use of knowledge must be uncovered and removed. Values, thinking, and behavior patterns promoting knowledge have to be spread and supported. Seufert et al. (1999) talk about different stages of the life cycle of a knowledge network. Depending on the stage, certain tasks must be fulfilled and various priorities must be set.

## CROSS-BORDER NETWORKS IN THE ALPINE REGION ON THE EXAMPLE OF ALPNET

The latest example of cross-border and international cooperation in the Alpine region is "AlpNet" (Alpine Economic Network), a network currently consisting of 51 tourism organizations and industrial companies (as at April 2002) interested in newly positioning the Alps. Their aim is to create a learning network as well as cross-border cooperation for Alpine marketing by implementing an information and communication platform, partly on the basis of the Internet (Fischer & Margreiter, 1999). While AlpNet is a knowledge-based platform for its members that are currently concentrating on exchanging experiences on the publication of market research data and on projects as well as on guidelines for positioning the brand "Alps," a separate business unit called Alpine Products & Services will provide commercial services such as marketing and distributing Alpine products in the future. In summary, it may be said that the project described above is a knowledge network that is the basis for a marketing and distribution network. Depending on the stage of the knowledge network, certain tasks must be fulfilled and different priorities must be set. The AlpNet project is only in its founding and structuring stage characterized by the following challenges: Search of appropriate partners, target agreement, establishment of streams of knowledge, achieving confidence, distribution of roles, definition of network regulation, and creation of adequate structures. Figure 1 shows the current management and corporation structure of AlpNet.

### AlpNet Member Survey 2001

In summer 2001, ICRET (International Center for Research and Education in Tourism) carried out a member survey of AlpNet at the University of Innsbruck (see Figure 2). ICRET is a network of scientists at different universities and research institutions as well as some provincial marketing organizations of the Alpine region aiming at applied and practical research for tourism economy. The main target of the study was to assess benefit profiles for the members and to establish a profile of core competencies for AlpNet. This is the reason why motives and needs are

FIGURE 1. Management and Corporate Structure of AlpNet (Fischer/Margreiter 1999)

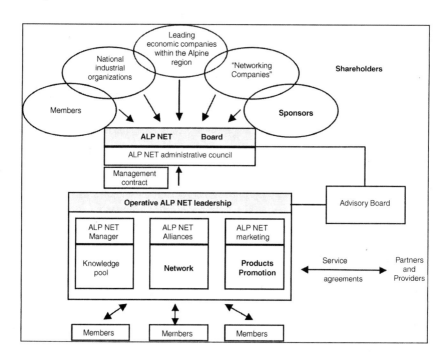

decisive for participating in the AlpNet project. The competencies contributed to the network, the significance of the various fields of cooperation, and the desired strategic direction of AlpNet were the main questions. Finally, members were asked how satisfied they were and to what extent their expectations were fulfilled in the first year.

## Methodology

The member survey is based on a standardized written questionnaire sent to all 51 AlpNet members. Hence, the study carried out is a census. Altogether 36 questionnaires were returned (70.59%). The evaluated questionnaires were spread across Austria (64%), Switzerland (22%), Italy (8%), and Germany (6%). The blocks of questions were codified in 4- or 5-point Likert scales. Mean values–if not indicated differently–refer to the arithmetic average of the characteristics of a 4-point Likert scale (1 =

FIGURE 2. Implications for Further Development of AlpNet (AlpNet member survey 2001)

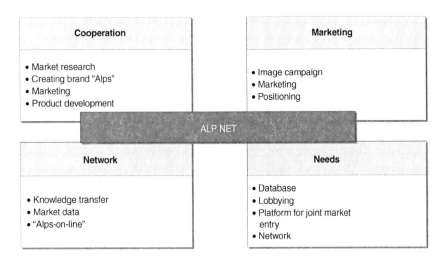

not important at all; 4 = very important). The reliability of the question blocks were confirmed by means of the Cronbach Alpha coefficient (values between $\alpha = 0.73$ and $0.88$).

A particularity of AlpNet is its heterogeneous member structure consisting of both tourism service carriers (e.g., tourism organizations and hotel cooperations) as well as other service carriers from fields other than tourism (e.g., industrial and service companies). The affinity of non-tourism organizations for local tourism was manifested in the conviction of private products being important for holidays in the Alps (at 80%) and in the wish to gain new customers as a result of cooperations with tourism companies and organizations (at 70%). The majority of participants (72%) are tourism organizations, mainly associations (52%) and corporate bodies under public law (40%). Tourism organizations are very heterogeneous themselves, as far as their number of members is concerned–varying from 2 to 9,000 members–as well as concerning their budget reaching from Euro 0.36 to Euro 43.6 Mio. When it comes to the number of employees in tourism organizations or to the number of overnight stays in the catchment area, figures strongly vary due to differences in organization size and structure. The evaluation was carried out on the basis of all participants, but also separated by tourism and non-tourism organizations.

## Motives and Needs

The first part of the survey deals with the question of what (general) needs and motives were essential for becoming a member at the AlpNet project. This question aimed at understanding people's motives, particularly regarding future member admission and attracting the attention of potential members.

Regarding general circumstances and developments, tourism organizations saw the main reason for becoming an AlpNet member in insufficient image campaigns (mean value 3.35), the poor positioning of the Alpine tourism (3.04), and the stagnation of tourism growth in the Alpine regions (3.00). For non-tourism organizations, on the contrary, minor professionalism in marketing the Alpine tourism by tourism organizations (3.70), insufficient product diversification, and the poor positioning of the Alpine tourism (3.20 each) were responsible for becoming a member.

The most important motive tied to business activity was the general exchange of experiences and knowledge with other AlpNet members (total mean value of 3.19). Moreover, tourism organizations consider cooperations attractive, particularly with regard to a general stronger presence on the tourism market (3.19). Non-tourism members rank the targeted exchange of plans and instructions of other members high (3.40). While tourism members evaluated the basic willingness to cooperate by other AlpNet members as rather modest (2.54), it is decisive for non-tourism members (3.13). They additionally expect to get partners for special projects and for joint product development as well as for receiving information on new target groups (3.20 each). The willingness to invest is clearly shown in these results. The focus is put on the exchange of knowledge, but clear differences in purpose are shown due to differences in the characteristics of the members. These partner asymmetries require a tense hierarchic structure for the further enlargement of AlpNet.

Main needs that should be fulfilled by AlpNet are the establishment of a database with access for AlpNet members, as well as lobbying in the field of economy and politics (3.00 each). Tourism organizations are especially interested in joint platforms for market entries in Europe (3.12). Non-tourism members, on the contrary, believe that the installation of networks which facilitate mutual finding (3.11) and the planning of joint activities (3.00) is more interesting.

Altogether, 66.7% of the study participants prefer a strong joint market entry of the destination Alps to a functioning network. When taking a closer look it is getting clear that mainly tourism members prefer a strong market entry (more than 80.0%), while non-tourism members (60.0%) think that a functioning network is far more important.

In summary, tourist organizations having joined the network seem to expect support in their marketing and positioning in order to overcome existing weaknesses. Non-tourism members appear to be more interested in enhancing their activities and learning. These diverging motives and expectations for entering the AlpNet point at the necessity of providing identifiable benefits for every member in order to maintain the network.

### Competencies

The majority of the respondents believe that the competencies they may contribute to AlpNet are experiences in public relations for specific target groups (3.06) and the planning and implementation of events (3.03). Some say that knowledge about the situation of the world tourism market is an essential competence (2.31). Tourism members only have a little experience in cooperating with non-tourism partners (2.35), yet they are used to cooperating with tourism partners (2.80) and with market research in particular (3.8). Non-tourism members, on the contrary, are characterized by their know-how in the field of target groups and their experience in marketing carried out for specific target groups (3.10 each).

Competencies considered essential for cooperation within the AlpNet are know-how on the general European tourism market and the experience in marketing carried out for specific target groups (2.80 each), as well as knowing the situation on the world tourism markets (2.77). An interesting difference between tourism and non-tourism members is that tourism members indicate those fields for cooperation where they lack competencies, whereas non-tourism members want to bring their fields of competence into the cooperation.

### Fields of Cooperation

These questions concentrated on central fields of cooperation in market research, marketing, and product development in the field of tourism. In general it can be said that all members show a high willingness to invest, i.e., a high readiness to engage themselves in several network activities and cooperation fields.

Regarding tourism market research, tourism organizations think that the image of the Alps (mean value 3.42), the discovering of concrete motives of a visitor spending his holidays in the Alps (3.38), and a sound knowledge of characteristics of current customer profiles in the Alps (3.23) to be important fields of cooperation. Non-tourism members, on the contrary, think that explorations of potential weak spots of activities (3.50), the discovering of existing weak points regarding activities (3.50), as well as intense analysis of customer behavior patterns on the spot (3.50) are important fields of cooperation for market research. Also in the framework of these potential fields of cooperation, the heterogeneity of the members is evident.

In the cooperation field of tourism marketing, tourism members believe that it is vital to establish the brand "Alps" (3.54), and that joint fundraising for market activities is also of great significance. Non-tourism members evaluate this field of cooperation lower in general, but they also rank the establishment of the brand "Alps" in the first place (2.70).

The analysis of tourism products in comparable destinations (total of 2.94), followed by the analysis of tourism products in alternative destinations (competitive products) (total of 2.86) rank first and second as a cooperation field for tourism product development. Initiating a working group for gathering ideas is seen as an important field of cooperation by non-tourism members (2.90), while tourism members rank it the least important field of cooperation (2.58).

The desired general strategic direction of AlpNet is clear. On the first place, members indicate product development and product innovation as the most important items for holidays in the Alps, followed by the establishment of new European target groups. Developing new markets and products outside of Europe are defined as less important. A striking difference may be seen in the processing of existing markets with existing products regarded as less important by non-tourism members compared to tourism members.

## Satisfaction with the AlpNet Project

The questionnaire pointed out that the AlpNet project is only in the structuring stage. Nevertheless, participants were asked whether they are satisfied with different fields in order to be better able to assess the current mood. The majority of the respondents are highly satisfied with the suggested AlpNet projects (3.32), as well as with the information on further steps taken by AlpNet (Member News) (3.12). Members were least content with the interrelated flow of information between the AlpNet members (2.35), as well as information on other AlpNet members (2.59). By comparing tourism and non-tourism members it can be stated that non-tourism members are most satisfied with information provided on the extended steps taken by AlpNet (3.78), while tourism members show highest satisfaction at suggested AlpNet projects (3.28). Here, it becomes obvious what items need further work for achieving a functioning network and for guaranteeing member commitment and contentment.

## *OUTLOOK*

The founding members of AlpNet are all from the tourism sector and are still those members with the highest willingness to invest. They represent the majority of the AlpNet board, which fulfills the functions of the hub firm in trying to move the network to the right strategic direction to establish the required stability and climate of confidence. The strong partner asymmetries from the founding stage of AlpNet will soon be regulated through a legal framework establishing a new hierarchic structure of the board and clearly defined decision processes within the network. With regard to the member heterogeneity, it is clear that hierarchy is needed in order to make the whole network work.

During the first year of AlpNet, many network partners were admitted because they manifested their interest in participating. Confidence and stability of a network are not a matter of size, but depend on the number and quality of contacts and communication among partners and on success. This can only be established over the years and is already taken charge of in the founding stage. The next years will show whether all partners will be able to guarantee stability and trust in the long term, if not there is also a possibility for the number of partners to decrease.

The AlpNet project is still is in its early stages. The member survey showed that the member heterogeneity–in particular regarding the different fields of competence–contains a big potential for the competitiveness of the (knowledge) network. But it also implies serious risks for AlpNet, e.g., if diverging member interests may not be linked and used in a way that everyone benefits from special advantages and synergies and that the value of the whole network may be increased. Particularly among tourism companies, network thinking seems to be less developed compared to non-tourism companies. Hence, it will be of decisive strategic importance to maintain the general positive mood full of expectations, in order to set specific action explicitly showing the individual benefits of each member, to establish a climate of confidence, and to enhance the exchange among members, as well as to increase their willingness to contribute their competencies into the network. This could be achieved by optimizing individual benefits of the knowledge pool or by making them visible. Furthermore, a focus should be put on innovation services in the field of product and market development, marketing, as well as high quality standards. This contribution shows the importance of a gradual approach when it comes to establishing a network as the basis for an international product development and marketing platform. Analyzing needs, motives, competencies, and fields of cooperation of current AlpNet members provides interesting facts on problems and perspectives for the future of the network, as well as for the admission of new members.

## REFERENCES

Augustyn, M. & Knowles, T. (2000): Performance of tourism partnerships: A focus on York, in: *Tourism Management*, Vol. 21, 341-351.

Bieger, Th. (1998): Reengineering Destination Marketing Organizations–The case of Switzerland, 33th TRC-Meeting, 15-18 May, Brijuni.

Bieger, Th. (2002): *Management von Destinationen*, 5th edition., Munich, Vienna: Oldenbourg.

Burgers, W.P., Hill, C.W. & Kim, W.C. (1993): A theory of global strategic alliances: The case of the global auto industry, in: *Strategic Management Journal*, Vol. 14, 419-432.

Campbell, A.J. & Wilson, D.T. (1996): Managed Networks: Creating Strategic Advantage, in: Iacobucci, D. (Ed.): *Networks in Marketing* (pp. 125-143), London: Sage.

Fischer, D. & Margreiter, J. (1999): Grenzüberschreitende Kooperation von Destinationen im Alpenraum, in: Pechlaner, H. & Weiermair, K. (Eds.): *Destinations- Management* (pp. 243-260), Vienna: Linde.

Gartner, W.C. & Lime, D.W. (Eds.) (2000): *Trends in Outdoor, Recreation, Leisure and Tourism*, Oxford: CAB International.

Grant, R. M., & Baden-Fuller, C. (2000): Knowledge and Economic Organization: An Application to the Analysis of Interfirm Collaboration, in: von Krogh, G., Nonaka, I. & Nishiguchi, T., *Knowledge Creation: A Source of Value* (pp. 113-150), London: Macmillan Press Ltd.

Håkansson, H. & Sharma, D.D. (1996): Strategic Alliances in a Network Perspective, in: Iacobucci, D. (Ed.): *Networks in Marketing* (pp. 108-124), London: Sage.

Håkansson, H., & Ford, D. (2002): How should companies interact in business networks?, in: *Journal of Business Research*, Vol. 55, No. 2, 133-139.

Hamel, G. (1991): Competition for competence and interpartner learning within international strategic alliances, in: *Strategic Management Journal*, Vol. 12, 83-103.

Inskeep, E. (1991): *Tourism Planning–An Integrated and Sustainable Development Approach*, New York: Van Nostrand Reinhold.

Jarillo, J.C. (1988): On Strategic Networks, in: *Strategic Management Journal*, Vol. 9, 31-41.

Jarillo, J.C. (1993): *Strategic networks: Creating the borderless organization*. Oxford: Butterworth-Heinemann.

Keller, P. (1996) (Eds.): Globalization and Tourism, Reports 46th AIEST-Congress, St-Gall: AIEST.

Laesser, Ch. & Jäger, S. (2001): Tourism in the new economy, in: Keller, P. & Bieger, Th. (Eds.): Tourism growth and global competition, Reports 51th AIEST-Congress (pp. 39-84), St-Gall, AIEST.

Malhotra, Y. (2000): *Knowledge management and virtual organizations*, London: Idea Group Publishing.

Miles, R.E. & Snow, C.C. (1995): The New Network Firm: A Spherical Structure Built on a Human Investment Philosophy, in: *Organizational Dynamics*, Spring 1995, 5-18.

Miles, R.E. & Snow, C.C. (1986): Organizations: New Concepts for New Forms, in: *California Management Review*, Vol. 28, 62-73.

Niederkofler, M. (1991): The evolution of strategic alliances. Opportunities for managerial influence, in: *Journal of Business Venturing*, Vol. 6, No. 2, 237-257.

Nonaka, I., & Takeuchi, H. (1995): *The knowledge creating company: How Japanese companies create the dynamics of innovation*, New York, Oxford: University Press.

Parkhe, A. (1991): Interfirm diversity, organizational learning and longevity in global strategic alliances, in: *Journal of International Business Studies*, Vol. 22, No. 6, 579-601.

Pechlaner, H. & Sauerwein, E. (2002): Strategy Implementation in the Alpine Tourism Industry, in: *International Journal of Contemporary Hospitality Management*, Vol. 14, No. 4, appears 2002.

Pechlaner, H. & Tschurtschenthaler, P. (2002): Tourism Policy, Tourism Organizations and Change Management in Alpine Regions and Destinations–A European Perspective, in: *Current Issues in Tourism*, appears 2002.

Riggers, B. (1998): *Value System Design: Unternehmenswertsteigerung durch strategische Unternehmensnetzwerke*. Wiesbaden: Deutscher Universitäts-Verlag.

Seufert, A., von Krogh, G., & Bach, A. (1999): Towards knowledge networking, in: *Journal of Knowledge Management*, Vol. 3, No. 3, 180-190.

Skyrme, D. (1999): *Knowledge Networking: Creating the Collaborative Enterprise*, Oxford: Butterworth-Heinemann.

Smeral, E. (1998): The impact of globalization on small and medium enterprises: new challenges for tourism policies in European countries, in: *Tourism Management*, Vol. 19, No. 4, 371-380.

Sydow, J. (1992): *Strategische Netzwerke. Evolution und Organisation*. Wiesbaden: Gabler.

Thomas, J.B. & Trevino, L.K. (1993): Information processing in strategic alliances: A multiple case approach, in: *Journal of Management Studies*, Vol. 30, 779-814.

von Krogh, G., Ichijo, K., & Nonaka, I. (2000): *Enabling knowledge creation*, New York, Oxford: University Press.

Wilkinson, I., & Young, L. (2002): On cooperating: Firms, relations and networks, in: *Journal of Business Research*, Vol. 55, No. 2, 123-132.

# Towards Using Knowledge Discovery Techniques in Database Marketing for the Tourism Industry

Vincent Cho

Paul Leung

**SUMMARY.** Given the trend that international corporations are utilizing various information systems for their daily activities, information on sales transactions together with corresponding customer profile is usually available in airlines and international hotel chains. This allows segments of customers to be drawn according to selected relevant demographic vari-

Vincent Cho is Assistant Professor, Hong Kong Polytechnic University, Department of Management (E-mail: msvcho@polyu.edu.hk). His main areas of interest and research include Data and Knowledge Management, Database Marketing, Artificial Intelligence, Ergonomics, Information Systems Management, Forecasting and Scheduling. He has been recently involved in stock marketing prediction. It was done by downloading electronic news from various well-known financial web sources. The downloaded textual data were then used to generate probabilistic rules for stock forecasting.

Paul Leung is Assistant Professor, Hong Kong Polytechnic University, Department of Hotel and Tourism Management (E-mail: hmpleung@polyu.edu.hk). His recent research interest is in the tourism development in Less Developed Countries and heritages tourism management and marketing, especially related to countries such as Cambodia and Egypt.

This research has been funded by (Grant G-YD49) The Hong Kong Polytechnic University, HKSAR, China.

[Haworth co-indexing entry note]: "Towards Using Knowledge Discovery Techniques in Database Marketing for the Tourism Industry." Cho, Vincent, and Paul Leung. Co-published simultaneously in *Journal of Quality Assurance in Hospitality & Tourism* (The Haworth Hospitality Press, an imprint of The Haworth Press, Inc.) Vol. 3, No. 3/4, 2002, pp. 109-131; and: *Knowledge Management in Hospitality and Tourism* (ed: Ricarda B. Bouncken and Sungsoo Pyo) The Haworth Hospitality Press, an imprint of The Haworth Press, Inc., 2002, pp. 109-131. Single or multiple copies of this article are available for a fee from The Haworth Document Delivery Service [1-800-HAWORTH, 9:00 a.m. - 5:00 p.m. (EST). E-mail address: docdelivery@haworthpress.com].

10.1300/J162v03n03_07

ables. This is referred to as Database Marketing, a new trend in marketing that makes use of information available in a company's database. The extracted information is also useful in planning marketing strategies, launching new products/services and defining market segmentation.

As databases in large corporations nowadays are getting large, sparser, more free-formatted and more dynamic, traditional statistical techniques may not be capable of extracting the encapsulated knowledge inside the databases. A new technical stream, data mining has been developed in Computer Science to deal with the complex task of extracting and managing any potential knowledge embedded inside databases. This paper introduces the common techniques in data mining, including decision tree classifiers, regression analysis, induction programming logic, and probabilistic rules. Suggestions are offered about how these techniques can be used in order to improve the engineering behind Database Marketing, which can help to promote niche markets in tourism. By utilizing its know-how in Database Marketing, a company can sharpen its competitiveness and build entry barriers for others. *[Article copies available for a fee from The Haworth Document Delivery Service: 1-800-HAWORTH. E-mail address: <docdelivery@haworthpress.com> Website: <http://www.HaworthPress.com> © 2002 by The Haworth Press, Inc. All rights reserved.]*

**KEYWORDS.** Database Marketing, data mining, tourism

## *INTRODUCTION*

The tourism industry, which includes the transportation, accommodation, catering, entertainment and retailing sectors, has grown significantly in recent decades, driven by the growth in the economy around the world. Tourism and the economy live in symbiosis and should be a win-win situation in which they benefit from one another. Nowadays, customers are getting more experienced, more sophisticated, are better informed and are thus more demanding. The ever-increasing demand for better customer service, the advancement in information technology, the expansion of new tourist destinations, and new forms of travel such as eco-tourism and cultural tourism, have changed the market landscape. For instance, new tour packages to Arctic or Antarctic destinations are increasing in supply to provide more variety for travellers.

This new trend will have impacts, both good and bad, on the economics, social values and culture, and infrastructure development in the high latitude regions such as New Zealand and Northern Europe. This surely means jobs and business opportunities. The growth rate, however, is far from satisfactory. One of the reasons for the low growth is that promotional materials are not targeted at the appropriate segment, so marketing efforts are simply wasted. This paper suggests a new technique for Database Marketing (DBM) to rectify the situation.

### Importance of Database Marketing

As suggested by Plog (1991), the simple rule of the game is to "know your market very well." The rationale is crystal clear and beyond argument. And perhaps it is just so simple and so beyond question that marketing managers have been caught unawares. Their pride in themselves and their establishment may have made them believe that they offered the best option for their client, and that don't need to look into the needs and wants profile of their customers. A database system, thus, can rectify the situation by, first of all, providing information about the customers, and secondly by instilling the important attitude that the business units have to update their understanding about their targets.

In addition, the market is ever-changing. Customer behavior, the market landscape, people's preferences, and fads are all changing continuously. And the pace is so fast that any perception that business managers hold about their target market(s) can become obsolete in the twinkling of an eye. A consolidated database and an effective data mining system, therefore, can be helpful in tracking this evolution.

Currently companies are utilizing the information system for their daily activities; information on sales transactions and customer profiles is usually available in large corporations such as airline, hotel chain or large tour operator. This is especially true when some large tour operator allows its travel agents to make transactions directly through its distributed network and the transactions are stored up in the centralized database owned by the large tour operator. These databases can serve the business by decreasing service time, minimizing wastage, increasing efficiency and saving money on the operational aspect. They also allow marketing managers to draw customer information according to whatever variable they choose. After analyzing the most suitable and potentially profitable customer profile for a particular tourism product, such as arctic adventure, the marketer can pull out of the database a list of customers/prospects with the required characteristics. Promotional material can then be targeted specifically to the needs of the identified group of customers. As a result, marketing costs can be reduced while response rates can be improved. Moreover, the customer responses can be recorded and be taken into account in future campaigns. A good database would thus increase the success rate by allowing service providers to render the service directly and quickly to customers, without the need of costly intermediaries.

### *Definition of Database Marketing*

The emergence of the concept of Database Marketing has become increasingly important in service industries especially in niche markets such as expeditions to the poles. Stan Rapp (1989) defines Database Marketing as "the ability of a company to use the vast potential of today's computer and telecommunications technology to drive customer-oriented programmes in a personalized, articulated and cost-effective manner." Fletcher and Wright (1990), on the other hand, defines Database Marketing from a more practical perspective as the mechanism that stores responses and adds other customer information, such as lifestyles, transaction history, etc., on an electronic database memory and uses it as a basis for long term customer loyalty programmes, facilitates contact and enables marketing planning.

As contended by Verhoef et al. (2002), Customer Relationship Marketing (CRM) is gaining its importance in modern business arena and Database Marketing embedded with data mining is to provide essential information for facilitating marketing decisions and CRM. Database Marketing assists management by grouping customers into clusters, which are homogeneous internally and heterogeneous mutually, so that marketing management can plan integrated communication strategies, design product offerings, determine pricing and utilize distribution networking accordingly.

According to Batra et al. (1995), Database Marketing serves the following logistic effects. First, it enables marketers to know more about the market and the various types of customers and their stages of readiness. Second, Database Marketing enables marketers to reach the right customer at the right time with the right offering. Third, Database Marketing is a growing mechanism that allows itself to grow and mature via its routine operations, and thus to develop into a even more powerful managerial tool. Fourth, enterprises can join together to share a common pool of data. Last but not least, the database mechanism serves customers by facilitating their decision with information.

Verhoef et al. (2002) argued that as a form of direct marketing, Database Marketing should subscribe the basic principles for direct marketing, viz., predictability through understanding of customer behavior, concentration through market segmentation, personalization through customization and immediacy through timely response.

## *Marketing Database*

Marketing database, which contains information about customers and markets, is one of the main assets of any marketing operation. The information on a marketing database has to come from somewhere. Database marketing is "learning by doing" (Shaw and Stone, 1988)–it provides most of the marketing information for a marketer. Each database marketing transaction/enquiry uses information, but it also generates new information. This is because database marketing campaigns ask for responses; and each response contains information. In this way, database marketing builds up a store of information about individual customers. The information must be managed in the most effective way. A computer system is crucial for organizing the information and making it available. According to Shaw and Stone (1988), there are two main objectives of computerizing the data. Firstly, to provide large volumes of segmented buyer and prospect data to help us develop profitable revenue streams through a data-driven dialogue with the target audience. Secondly, to enable the marketing manager to analyze and segment the target audience in order to determine strategy. The marketing information system requires mainly summary, aggregated or sample data, not individual customer data. The database marketer, on the other hand, needs information on the activity and characteristics of individual buyers and prospects.

If a database is to contribute fully to marketing operations then, according to Shaw and Stone (1988), it should have the following characteristics:

1. Each actual or potential customer is identified as an individual record on the marketing database.
2. Each customer's record contains not only identification and access information but also a range of marketing information.
3. The information is available to the company during the process of each transaction with the customer, to enable it to decide how to respond to the customer's needs.
4. The database is used to record responses of customers to company initiatives.

5. The information is also available to marketing policy makers to enable them to make decisions about the product and marketing mix most suitable for each target market identified.
6. In large travel operators, selling many products to each customer, the database is used to ensure that the approach to the customer is co-ordinated and a consistent approach developed.
7. The information built up, over time, on the database will gradually reduce the need for market research. Marketing campaigns are derived such that the response of customers to the campaign provides the information that the company is looking for.
8. Marketing management automation is developed to handle the vast volume of information generated by Database Marketing. Although no tourism-related corporation has yet achieved this level of sophistication, many are adopting it as their goal.

Furthermore, an effective database management system is not limited to its logistic operation of building up a database but to enhance management effectiveness and efficiency. That means it is part of the management/marketing information system. In general, a fully integrated database marketing system, as shown in Figure 1, consists of four components, namely (1) marketing database, (2) financial and operational systems, (3) marketing and sales systems, and (4) company planning. Marketing database stores customer-related records and information. The financial and operational systems include order entry, billing, and inventory control. The marketing sales systems relate to campaign planning, sales forecasting, sales support, direct mail, and sales force management. Lastly, company planning formulates the strategic planning, product planning and research and development.

Although technology is a powerful element in this system, it should not dictate the system. After all, it is not the technology but its abilities to provide the necessary information that matters. Information management, however, is beyond the scope of this paper. The following discussion will still focus on the construction of Database Marketing and the corresponding data mining technique.

### Sources of Data

A database marketing system normally uses most of the customer information available within a company, but organizes it differently from the operations databases from which much of this customer information

FIGURE 1. Fully Integrated Database Marketing

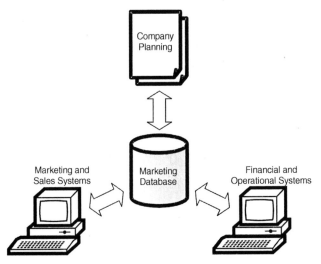

is likely to be drawn. There are two types of data sources, internal and external. Internal data sources include order records, service reports, complaints, application forms, market research, etc. External data is gotten from outside the company, including compiled lists and classificatory data such as census data. External lists are often classified into mail responsive and compiled. Mail responsive lists consist of anyone who uses the post for transactions which could be carried out in some other way. Compiled lists are those committed to cover particular kinds of people. Lists can be sourced from list brokers who often act as agents for list owners. They also can be sourced from directories and by research.

The quality of the data drawn from a database depends mainly on how up-to-date the source data are; and whether they contain the detail needed to access the right individuals. Databases get out-of-date quickly. People change addresses and jobs. Companies move, new companies are set-up and companies go out of existence. Errors in fulfillment records occur, through commission and omission. This is why audits must be undertaken. The quality of the data is measured by results of the last audit carried out on them. It should be possible to carry out some quality checks via testing.

## Current Applications of Database Marketing

Database Marketing, an increasingly important area in customer behavior analysis, is being adopted by many international corporations, such as American Airlines, American Express, Time Life, Austin Rover, British Telecom, Bank of America, Derbyshire Building Society, Automobile Association, De Vere Hotels, etc. (Fletcher et al., 1991; Rapp and Collins, 1987; Taylor and Oake, 1991). In Hong Kong, the Hong Kong Telecom provides point-to-point on-line service to every household starting from late 1997. Through a television at home, customers can access a range of self-selected entertainment programmes, on-line shipping and banking facilities. The company plans to make use of the database by recording the activities of individual customers for marketing. Similarly, Internet service providers in Hong Kong also keep track of the activities of their customers and are moving towards this new trend on Database Marketing.

## Obstacles and Barriers to Implementation of DBM

According to Fletcher et al. (1990), and Stone and Shaw (1987; 1988), Database Marketing can be used to develop new and unique products or services, change the basis of competition, build barriers to entry by competitors, and strengthen customer relationships. The implementation of database marketing systems has become a priority in many industries. However, success is not guaranteed. Fletcher et al. (1991) conducted a study which revealed the major obstacles to the implementation of DBM. Their sample consisted of the largest 180 life and general insurance companies (by gross premium income), the largest 44 building societies (by total assets) and the largest 28 banks (by net interest income and other operating income) in UK. The results, as shown in Figure 2, revealed that the high cost of development, the high fragmented systems and the data quality are the top three most prominent barriers with mean scores of 4.99, 4.92 and 4.82 on a 7-point Likert-type scale ranging from most important barrier (point 7) to least important barrier (point 1) respectively. Although the study is not about the tourism industry, there are at least two commonalities between financial market and tourism market DBM: their complexity and the large amount of information to process.

FIGURE 2. Barriers to Implementing DBM

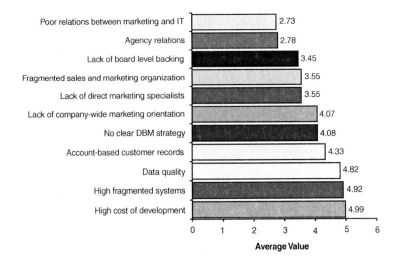

A New Approach for Database Marketing

Verhoef et al. (2002), however, argued that most of the recent work on Database Marketing focuses on data mining. Data mining, which began in the 1990s, is generally defined in Cho (1998), Smyth et al. (1996), and Wüthrich (1995) as "the nontrivial extraction of implicit, previously unknown, and potentially useful information from data. This implicit information which we call knowledge is hidden in the databases and is usually in the form of relationships among data items. These relationships may be in the form of functional, or partial functional dependencies. Their discovery analysis and characterization may involve the use of various techniques." This new technology is particularly helpful to Database Marketing as there should be some unknown, usually non-linear, patterns in data that cannot be easily found by conventional statistical methods.

Data mining differs from machine learning, as the nature of data tends to be dynamic, incomplete, redundant, noisy, sparse and very large (Chen et al., 1996). Some commonly-used techniques in data mining include decision trees, regression analysis, inductive logic rules and neural nets. However, each technique has its own strength and weakness, making it applicable in only certain problem domains (Wüthrich, 1995). Furthermore, there is a growing need for data mining tools to cater for probabilistic and temporal data, as real-world problems are usually fuzzy (not strictly black and white) and closely related to time (Wüthrich, 1995).

## DATA MINING TECHNIQUES

In order to provide a fundamental overview, a hypothetical database is illustrated to assist our elaboration of those data mining techniques (see Figure 3). The corresponding data can be collected through some survey on travellers or sales transactions of flight tickets.

This paper outlines major principles of some major classification techniques such as decision tree, statistical analysis, nearest neighbor learning, inductive logic programming, probabilistic rules and neural network. Their strengths, limitations, applications, and references are summarized in Table 1.

### Nearest Neighbor

One way to classify a case is to recall a similar case whose class is known and to predict that the new case will have the same class. This is the philosophy underlying nearest neighbor systems which classify unseen cases by referring to similar and remembered cases. It is an example of the lazy learning paradigm. Although many variants of nearest neighbor learning algorithms exist, these algorithms, generally speaking, store all (or selected) training examples, and utilize a similarity (or distance) function to measure the similarity (or distance) of a testing ex-

FIGURE 3. Hypothetical Database

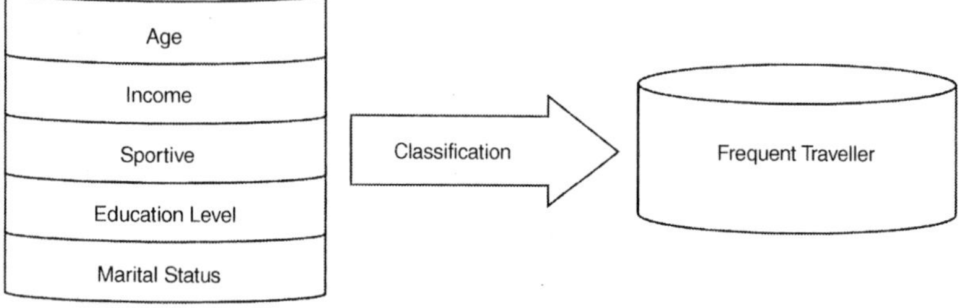

TABLE 1. Strength and Limitations of Data Mining Techniques

| Data Mining Technique | Strengths | Limitations | Applications |
|---|---|---|---|
| Nearest Neighbour (Ada et al., 1991; Dasarathy, 1991) | Easy implementation. Fast training. | Hard to interpret for non-ordinal attributes. May be influenced by unimportant attributes. | Spatial analysis of occupation floors (Whallon, 1974). Clustering of tourist attractions (Vasiliadis and Kobotis, 1999). |
| Decision Trees and Inductive Logic Programming (Breiman et al., 1984; Kass, 1980; Quinlan, 1987a; Quinlan, 1993) | Relatively easy to interpret. | Weak in handling continuous attributes. Difficult to handle missing data. | Patient image pre-fetching (Wei et al., 2001). Holiday choice behavior (Bargeman et al., 1999). |
| Statistical Discriminator (Hunt, 1975; Shepherd et al., 1988) | Model building is very fast. Almost optimal for linear model. | Not suitable to model non-linear relationships. | Biological application (Shelperd et al., 1988). Hotel customers behavior (Morrison et al., 2000). |
| Neural Networks (Aleksander and Morton, 1990; Beale and Jackson, 1990; Wasserman, 1989) | Little assumption for modelling. Effective in learning cases that contain noisy, incomplete or contradictory data. | Lack explanation capabilities, Training process is slow. | Engineering application (Corcoran and Lowery, 1995). Assessment of business partners (Lau et al., 2001). Predicting market responses (van Wezel and Baets, 1995). Travel Market Segmentation (Mazanec, 1993). |
| Probabilistic Rules (Wüthrich, 1993; 1995; 1997) | Comprehensible. | Training time is exponential to the number of rules to be generated. | Web-mining (Cho, 1998). |

ample with the stored training examples when predicting the class of the testing example. That is, they do not induce a concept description during the training process, as there is no training process. Instead, they predict the testing period by relying on the training examples. A popular example is $k$-nearest neighbor ($k$-NN) algorithm (Dasarathy, 1991). It determines the classification of a testing example by selecting a set of $k$ closest training examples–normally the majority class of the $k$ selected training examples. The distance function of nearest neighbor (NN) algorithms may take the following form:

$$dist(x, x') = \sum (x_i - x_i')^2 \tag{1}$$

where $x$ is the testing example, $x'$ is the training example, and $x_i$ and $x_i'$ are the normalized values of the $i$th attribute.

For example, $x_i$ may represent the normalized values of essential characteristics of travellers, such as marital status, age, income and level of education. The distance definition can be used to estimate the cluster center of a set of objects. Using the entropy concept, several previously unknown classes in classifying travellers can be identified.

## Decision Tree

A decision tree classifies objects hierarchically. It may be either a leaf identified by a class name, or a structure of the form:

$$C_1 : D_1$$
$$C_2 : D_2$$
$$\ldots$$
$$\ldots$$
$$C_n : D_n$$

where the $C_i$ s are mutually exclusive and exhaustive logical conditions and the $D_i$ s are themselves decision trees as shown in Figure 4.

FIGURE 4. Decision Tree

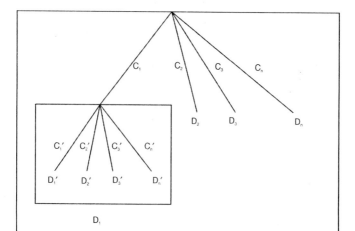

The set of conditions involves only one of the attributes, each condition being:

$$A < T \ or \ A \geq T$$

for a continuous attribute $A$, where $T$ is a threshold, or:

$$A = V \ or \ A \ in \ \{V_i\}$$

for a discrete attribute $A$, where $V$ is one of its possible values and $\{V_i\}$ is a subset of them. Such a decision tree is used to classify a case as follows. If the tree is a leaf, we simply determine the case's class to be the one nominated by the leaf. If the tree is a structure, we find the single condition $C_i$ that holds for this case and continue with the associated decision tree.

The following is a decision tree generated from a database in a travel agent (see Figure 5). The attributes, travel frequency and age, are the two most relevant attributes that would be extracted from numerous attributes existing in the database for the purpose of characterizing the po-

FIGURE 5. Decision Tree on the Potential of a Traveller Joining a Tour to the Poles

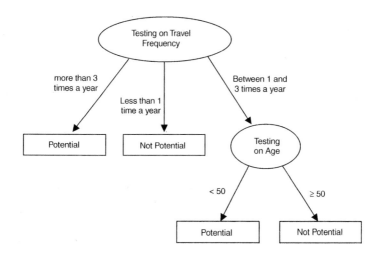

tential of a person joining a package tour to the poles. Here a person is classified as either potential or not potential.

## Statistical Discriminator

Statistics has given rise to a multitude of classification methods, many of which are presented concisely in Hunt (1975). As a general rule, however, statistical techniques tend to focus on tasks in which all the attributes have continuous or numeric values. Many of the techniques are parametric that assume a particular model and then find appropriate values for the model's parameters from the data. For instance, a linear classifier assumes that a class can be expressed as a linear combination of the attribute values. Based on that assumption, it finds the particular linear combination that gives the best fit over the training cases. Maximum likelihood classifiers often assume that attribute values are normally distributed and use the training data to determine the distribution means, variances, and co-variances (Shepherd et al., 1988). The most popular technique is regression analysis, especially linear regression analysis.

Suppose a discriminant function is generated as follows:

$$travel\_frequency(X) = 0.05\ age(X) + 0.0001\ income(X) \qquad (2)$$

and the threshold to determine a frequent traveller is 2.8 (number of travel per annum). Now suppose Mary is a 24 year old girl with annual income of ten thousand. According to equation (2), the predicted travel frequency of Mary is $0.05 \times 24 + 0.0001 \times 10,000 = 2.2$; thus she will be classified as an infrequent traveller.

## Inductive Logic Programming

Inductive Logic Programming is a technique that induces logical relationships based on fact data and background knowledge. All the fact data, background knowledge and induced concepts are represented by restricted program clauses. A programme clause has the following form:

$$p(X_1, \ldots, X_n) \leftarrow L_1, \ldots, L_m \qquad (3)$$

where $L_i$, $i = 1, 2, \ldots, m$, the body of a clause, is a conjunction of positive literals $q_i(Y_1, \ldots, Y_k)$ and/or negative literals *not* $q_i(Y_1, \ldots, Y_k)$ such that

$q_i$, $i = 1, 2, \ldots, m$, is the name of the $i$th literal and $Y_j$, $j = 1, 2, \ldots, k$, is its $j$th argument. $p$ is the name of the goal predicate and $X_i$, $i = 1, 2, \ldots, n$, is its $i$th argument.

This representation allows learning to be considered as logic program synthesis (De Raedt et al., 1993; Quinlan, 1990). For illustration, given the demographic data from a customer database, they are as follows:

*young(peter), young(steven), young(vincent), young(mary), ...*

*high_income(mary), high_income(vincent), ...*

*sportive(peter), sportive(vincent), ...*

*frequent_traveller(vincent), ....*

They indicate whether a person is young, rich, sporty, or a frequent traveller. Based on the above facts, with the Inductive Logic Programming, knowledge such as *frequent_traveller(X) ← high_income(X) and frequent_traveller(X) ← sportive(X)* would be induced automatically. This means that a person would be a frequent traveller if he or she is *high_income* or *sportive*. These rules represent the dependence between the four attributes *frequent_traveller, high_income, sportive,* and *young* in a customer database. The definition of *young, high_income, sportive* or *frequent_traveller* may affect the induced result and the corresponding interpretation. This simplified example is only for illustration purposes. The actual application of Inductive Logic Programming is more complicated.

### *Neural Network*

Neural networks (Aleksander and Morton, 1990; Beale and Jackson, 1990) are computing devices inspired by the function of nerve cells in the brain. They are composed of many parallel, interconnected computing units. Each of these performs a few simple operations and communicates results to its neighboring units. In contrast to conventional computer programs where step-by-step instructions are provided to perform a particular task, neural networks can learn to perform tasks by a process of training on many different examples.

Typically, the nodes of a neural network are organized into layers with each node in one layer having a connection to each node in the next layer as shown in Figure 6. Associated with each connection is a weight and each node has an activation value. During pattern recognition, each node operates as a simple threshold device. A node sums all the weighted inputs (multiplying the connection weight by the state of the previous layer node) and then applies a (typically non-linear) activation function as shown in Figure 7.

It is the values of the weights and the topology that determine the types of patterns a neural network can recognize. Figure 8 shows a neural network example model of predicting travel frequency of travellers based on their age, income and sportiveness.

### Probabilistic Rule

Probabilistic rule (Wüthrich, 1996) is an extension of first-order rule with the ability to handle uncertain or weighted facts. It is developed on the natural class of disjunctive probabilistic concepts and satisfies the laws of axiomatic probability theory. Probabilistic rule (Wüthrich, 1995) assumes a set of facts, each associated with a strength/probability in the closed real interval between zero and one. The domain knowledge and the induced knowledge are in the form of rules with certain strengths or probabilities. This technique can be further modified to handle the categorical data (Cho and Wüthrich, 1996), and has been proved to be quite successful in this aspect. The following example gives a basic outline of this technique.

Assume that Peter and Mary are friends. The strength of their friendship is *0.88*. The corresponding sportiveness can be scaled as *0.8* and *0.7* re-

FIGURE 6. Neural Network

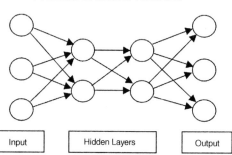

FIGURE 7. Neuron Mechanism

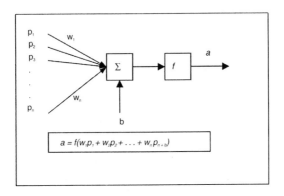

FIGURE 8. Neural Network Example Model

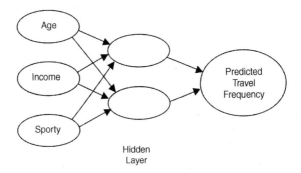

spectively. These facts can be coded to be *{friendship(Peter,Mary) = 0.88, sportiveness(Peter) = 0.8, sportiveness(Mary) = 0.7}*, assuming that the following rules, with a number attached indicating the corresponding strength, are induced from the Probabilistic Datalog Technique.

$$frequent\_traveller(x) \leftarrow friendship(x, y), frequent\_traveller(y) \quad :0.65 \quad (4)$$

$$frequent\_traveller(x) \leftarrow sportiveness(x) \quad :0.42 \quad (5)$$

The term *frequent_traveller(X)* will indicate the strength of a person *X* to be a frequent traveller. According to the rules (4) and (5), the strength of *frequent_traveller(Peter)* is $0.8 \times 0.42 = 0.336$ and the strength of *frequent_traveller(Mary)* is $0.7 \times 0.42 + (0.8 \times 0.42) \times 0.88 \times 0.65 - (0.7 \times 0.42) \times (0.8 \times 0.42 \times 0.88 \times 0.65) = 0.43$.

## POSSIBLE APPLICATIONS OF DATABASE MARKETING IN TOURISM INDUSTRY

Tourism is a huge but young industry. The customer base is big and their behaviors are rapidly revolving. This ever-changing nature of the market presented the greatest challenge to marketers of touristic products and that is to access the desire and demand changes. Consolidated database provides a mean to the problem. The archive of behavioral pattern in terms of choices and consumption decision stores resources that can monitor and predict market changes. Currently, however, customer databases in large tourism related corporations are usually large, incomprehensible and spare, and a lot of unknown patterns about customers are simply ignored. It can be seen that all techniques used in data mining would be applicable to Database Marketing. An appropriate definition of distance in measuring customer characteristics and the class identification technique could be applied to identifying unknown clusters. These discovered clusters might represent certain interesting classes representing different segments in the market. For example, the enquiry for information regarding new destination might present new market opportunities. The past purchases decisions could be useful input for clustering different groups of travellers into segments for more effective market communications. Travel agents and organizations, therefore, can be more target oriented and effective in cultivating businesses for niche markets, such as tours to the poles, high latitude or altitude regions.

Moreover, the details of individual clusters can be studied using the data mining techniques such as regression analysis, decision tree, probabilistic rules, or neural network. Once the relevant attributes for each cluster are located, new marketing strategies can be planned to enhance a company's competitive edge. For example, if potential correlation between information search mode and destination choices can be identified, a more effective communication program can be in place.

Database marketing embedded with data mining techniques is of critical value to the tourism industry owing to its fragmented nature, the widely dispersed customers, the heterogeneous behaviors of tourists, the rapidly changing market landscape and the complex contextual environment of the industry. In other words, data mining enables managers to know what is unknown and unable to investigate in the past.

Any importance performance indicator such as profit margin, sales volume or stock price can be analyzed using probabilistic rules or regression analysis. The findings can provide a greater understanding of relevant factors affecting these key performance indicators, and will certainly help management in their decision-making about marketing issues such as sales force control, forecasting/monitoring sales and cost savings.

Furthermore, a database marketing strategy to be effective requires inputs of information. An effective database logistic enables critical information to be disseminated to the users at the right time, in the right format and with the least troubles. A database, however, cannot serve the purpose. An effective system, which requires a holistic approach to information management, is critical. It could be a nuisance to the management in the process of development but it is a critical step towards more effective management. The exercise, therefore, can be regarded as a means to upgrade the managerial mentality of the company and to formalize the information logistic framework.

Data mining also initiates more creative and powerful use of data and information. The use of integrated information system/database is gaining its popularity. This huge database, however, has not been fully functional. The reports being generated became the barrier or boundary to the use of these invaluable information. Data mining, on the other hand, allows individual managers to manoeuvre the database to assist his/her decisions and the cultivation of competitive merits. To achieve this requires a study of the existing information base of a company, and its capability to support existing marketing activities. It also requires managers' ability to spot opportunity and take actions accordingly.

For more concrete illustrations, the Los Angeles-based Australian Tourist Commission (ATC) has successfully achieved an integrated database marketing approach (Robinson, 1997). It maintains a single data warehouse for all customer data. By facilitating data mining techniques, it can quickly and accurately determine which travel agents and consumers are responding to its advertising effort and from which sources, such as television, cable, direct mail, etc. This ability helps ATC to produce a suite of tailored reports and choose better in its media buying. It also enables the organization to tailor travel packages and marketing campaigns to meet respondents' immediate and long-range needs and interests (Robinson, 1997).

Aruba, an island with a windward coast on the Caribbean, has been successfully using a marketing database system for years to convert approximately twice as many of its inquirers into actual visitors. With the program, Hug-and-Hold Inquirer Conversion and Repeat System, Aruba has doubled its 12 percent inquirer conversion rate to 26 percent (Bono, 1995).

## CONCLUSION

These days, corporate organizations, governments and scientific communities are overwhelmed with an influx of data that is routinely stored in on-line databases. A new technology in the 1990s, data mining, has been developed to analyze and extract meaningful patterns in a timely way. This research area promises handsome payoffs in many businesses and scientific organizations. Besides providing a preliminary understanding of data mining, this paper suggests possible discoveries using data mining and how it can be applied to Database Marketing development in the tourism industry.

In order to be successful in the tourism industry, or in any other industry, one must be a master of the concept of marketing. The needs, wants and demands of potential and existing customers must be well understood by the marketers (Berry, 1994). Proper planning and execution of marketing programmes can help to build a long-term competitive advantage for a company. These tasks consist of the determination of specific target markets and manipulating the marketing-mix elements to best satisfy the needs of the individual target market. To proceed with these tasks, guest history data can be extracted from the existing customer database, which stores huge amounts of sales transaction data with corresponding customer profiles. Advanced techniques in data mining are used to manipulate the extracted data and to give management an edge in learning more about their customers. This customer database can also be used to build customer loyalty (Robinson and Kearney, 1994). As data collection systems become more accepted and as databases contain more integrative information, data mining, a possible tool for Database Marketing, will be more important in promoting niche marketing.

# REFERENCES

Aha, D.W., Kibler, D. and Albert, M.K. (1991). Instance-Based Learning Algorithms. *Machine Learning*, 6(1): 37-66.

Aleksander, I. and Morton, H. (1990). *Introduction to Neural computing*. North Oxford Press.

Batra, R. et al. (eds.) (1995). *The New Direct Marketing: How to Implement a Profit-Driven Database Marketing Strategy*. Burr Ridge, IL: Irwin.

Bargeman, B., Joh, C.H., Timmermans, H. and Van der Waerden, P. (1999). Correlates of tourist vacation behavior: A combination of CHAID and loglinear logit analysis. *Tourism Analysis*, 4(2): 83-93.

Beale, R. and Jackson, T. (1990). *Neural Computing–An Introduction*. Bristol: Adam Hilger.

Berry, J. (1994). Database Marketing. *Business Week*, September.

Bono, J.J. (1995). Marketing Database Heats Up Tourism For Sunny Aruba. *Direct Marketing*, October, 18-21.

Breiman, L., Friedman, J.H., Olshen, R.A. and Stone, C.J. (1984). *Classification and Regression Trees*. Belmont, CA: Wadsworth.

Catlett, J. (1991). *Megainduction. PhD Thesis, Basser Department of Computer Science*. University of Sydney.

Chen, M.S., Han, J. and Yu, P. (1996). Data Mining: An Overview from Database Perspective. *IEEE Trans. On Knowledge and Data Engineering*.

Cho, V. (1998). World Wide Web resources. *Annals of Tourism Research*, 25, 518-521.

Cho, V., and Wüthrich, B. (1996). Consistent Prediction for Categorical Data. *Ninth International Symposium on Methodologies for Intelligent Systems*, June, 9-13, Zakopane. Poland.

Cohen, W. (1995). Fast Effective Rule Induction. *12th Int Conf on Machine Learning*, pp. 80-89.

Corcoran, P., Lowery, P. (1995). Neural network applications in multisensor systems. *Sensor Review*, 15(4), 15-18.

Dasarathy, B. (1991). *Nearest Neighbor (NN) Norms: NN Pattern Classification Techniques*. Los Alamitos, CA: IEEE Computer Society Press.

De Raedt, L. and Lavrac, N. and Dzeroski, S. (1993). Multiple Predicate Learning. *Proc Int Joint Conf on AI (IJCAI)*, 1037-1042.

Desai, C., Wright, G. and Fletcher, K. (1998). Barriers to successful implementation of Database Marketing: A cross-industry study, *International Journal of Information Management*, 18(4), pp. 265-276.

Egghe, L. (1992). Duality aspects of the Gini index for general information production processes. *Information Processing and Management*, 28(1), 35-44.

Fletcher, K., Wheeler, C. and Wright, J. (1990). The Role and Status of UK Database Marketing. *The Quarterly Review of Marketing*, 16(1).

Fletcher, K., Wheeler, C. and Wright, J. (1991). Database Marketing: A Channel, a Medium, or a Strategic Approach? *International Journal of Advertising*, 10, 117-127.

Hunt, E.B. (1975). *Artificial Intelligence*. New York: Academic Press.

Kass, G.V. (1980). An Exploratory Technique for Investigating Large Quantities of Categorical Data. *Applied Statistics*, 29, 119-127.

Lau, H.C.W., Lee, W.B. and Lau, P.K.H. (2001). Development of an intelligent decision support system for benchmarking assessment of business partners. *Benchmarking*, 8(5), 376-395.

Mazanec, J.A. (1993). Exporting Eurostyles to the USA. *International Journal of Contemporary Hospitality Management*, 5(4), 3-9.

Morrison, A.M., Bose, G. and O'Leary, J.T. (2000). Can statistical modeling help with data mining?: A database marketing application for US hotels. *Journal of Hospitality and Leisure Marketing*, 6(4), 91-110.

Nash, E.L. (1995). *Direct Marketing: Strategy, Planning, and Execution*. McGraw-Hill, New York.

Nilsson, N.J. (1965). *Learning Machines*. New York: McGraw-Hill.

Pagalo, G. and Haussler, D. (1990). Boolean Feature Discovery in Empirical Learning. *Machine Learning*, 5(1), 71-100.

Plog, S.C. (1991). *Leisure Travel: Making it a Growth Market . . . Again!* New York: Wiley.

Quinlan, J.R. (1987a). Simplifying Decision Trees. *International Journal of Man-Machine Studies*, 27, 221-234.

Quinlan, J.R. (1987b). Generating Production Rules From Decision Trees. *Int Joint Conf. on Artificial Intelligence*, 304-307.

Quinlan, J.R. (1990). Learning Logical Definitions from Relations. *Machine Learning*, 5, 239-266.

Quinlan, J.R. (1993). *Programs for Machine Learning*. San Mateo, CA: Morgan Kaufmann.

Rapp, S. (1989). So What Is Direct Marketing Anyway. *Direct Response*, 27, July.

Rapp, S. and Collins, T. (1987). *Maxi-marketing*. McGraw-Hill. New York.

Robinson, R. and Kearney, T. (1994). Database Marketing for Competitive Advantage in the Airline Industry. *Journal of Travel & Tourism Marketing*, 3(1), 65-81.

Robinson, R. (1997). 1:1 marketing: An integrated strategy to reach customers. *Telemarketing & Call Center Solutions*, 15(11), 66-74.

Shaw, R. and Stone, M. (1987). Database Marketing for Competitive Advantage. *Long Range Planning*, 20(2), 12-20.

Shaw, R. and Stone, M. (1988). *Database Marketing*. Gower, Aldershot.

Shepherd, B., Piper J. and Rutovitz, D. (1988). Comparison of ACLS and Classical Linear Methods in a Biological Application. In Hayes, J.E., Michie, D., and Richards, J. (ed.), *Machine Intelligence*, 11 (pp. 423-434). Oxford, UK: Oxford University Press.

Smyth, P., Fayyad, U., Piatetsy-Shapiro and Uthurusamy, R. (1996). *Advances in Knowledge Discovery and Data Mining*. MIT Press. Cambridge.

Stanfill, C. and Waltz, D. (1986). Toward Memory-Based Reasoning. *Communications of the ACM*, 29(12): 1213-1228.

Taylor, J. and Oake, J. (1991). Maximizing Financial Services: Sophisticated Database Marketing. *International Journal of Bank Marketing*, 9(2).

Verhoef, P.C., Spring, P.N., Hoekstra, J.C. and Leeflang, P.S.H. (uncorrected proof) (2002). The commercial use of segmentation and predictive modeling technique for database marketing in the Netherlands, *Decision Support System*, 965.

van Wezel, M.C. and Baets, W.R.J. (1995). Predicting market responses with a neural network: The case of fast moving consumer goods, *Marketing Intelligence & Planning*, 13(7), 23-30.

Vasiliadis, C.A. and Kobotis, A. (1999). Spatial analysis: An application of nearest-neighbor analysis to tourism locations in Macedonia. *Tourism Management*, 20(1), 141-148.

Wasserman, P.D. (1989). *Neural Computing: Theory and Practice*. New York: Van Nostrand Reinhold.

Whallon, Jr., R. (1974). Spatial Analysis of Occupation Floor II: The Application of Nearest Neighbor Analysis. *American Antiquity*, 39(1), 16-34.

Wei, C.P., Hu, P.J.H. and Sheng, O.R.L. (2001). A knowledge-based system for patient image pre-fetching in heterogeneous database environments–modeling, design, and evaluation, *Information Technology in Biomedicine, IEEE Transactions*, 5(1), 33-45.

Weiss, S.M. and Kulikowshi, C.A. (1991). *Computer Systems that Learn: Classification and Prediction Methods from Statistics, Neural Nets, Machine Learning and Expert Systems*. San Mateo, CA: Morgan Kaufmann.

White, A.P. and Liu, W.Z. (1997). Statistical Properties of Tree-Based Approaches to Classification. in Nakhaeizadeh, G., and Taylor, C.C. (eds), *Machine Learning and Statistics*. John Wiley & Sons Inc., New York, 1997.

Wüthrich, B. (1993). On the Learning of Rule Uncertainties and Their Integration into Probabilistic Knowledge Bases. *Journal of Intelligent Information Systems*, 1(2), 245-264.

Wüthrich, B. (1995). Toward a Formal Framework for Comparing KD Techniques. *Proceedings of the DOOD'95 Post-Conference Workshops*, Dec., 9-16, Singapore.

Wüthrich, B. (1996). Probabilistic Knowledge Bases. *IEEE Transactions of Knowledge and Data Engineering*, 7(5), 691-698.

Wüthrich, B. (1997). Discovery Probabilistic Decision Rules. *Int. Journal of Intelligent Systems in Accounting, Financial & Management*.

Wüthrich, B., Tong, W.C. and Sankaran, K. (1995). Temporal and Probabilistic, Deductive and Object-Oriented Query Language. *Proceedings of the DOOD'95 Post-Conference Workshops*, Dec., 61-68, Singapore.

# Index

Accor hotel group, 53-54
Accumulation, knowledge, 37-38
Acquisition, knowledge, 36-37
Airline industry, 66-72
    knowledge management, 69-71
    situation, 66-69
Alpine tourism. *See* AlpNet
AlpNet, 89-107. *See also* AlpNet
    member survey; Cross-border
    knowledge networks
    alpine tourism changes, 90-92
    as cross-border knowledge network,
      98-104
    non-tourism organizations in,
      100-101
    outlook for, 104-105
    vs. cooperative marketing, 91-92
AlpNet member survey 2001, 98-104
    competencies, 102
    fields of cooperation, 102-103
    methodology, 99-100
    motives and needs, 101-102
    satisfaction with project, 103-104
American Airlines, 116
American Express, 116
Application layer, 79
Arthur D. Little High Performance
    Model, 61-66
Artifacts, organizational, 44
Asymmetric information, 17-20
    forms of, 17-19
    reducing risks of, 19-20
Asymmetries, partner, 95
Austin Rover, 116

Back office operations, 18-19
Bank of America, 116

Berlin University of Technology
    Knowledge Cafe system,
      80-84
Best Western International, Inc., 34-35
Brandenburg University of Technology
    Cottbus, 1-4, 25-39
British Telecom, 116
Brokers, network, 93

Circles, knowledge, 52-53
Codification, 28, 43-44
Codified vs. personalized knowledge
    transfer, 42-45
Cognitive mapping, 12-17
    asymmetric information, 17-20
    concept of, 12-13
    organizational theory and, 13-15
    tourism-specific aspects, 16-17
Cognitive understanding of
    knowledge, 28
Collaboration services, 79
Collective vs. individual knowledge,
    29
Confidence, as network requirement,
    95
Constructivist understanding of
    knowledge, 28
Controlling knowledge, 38-39
Cooperative/competitive relationships,
    6-7
Cooperative marketing, 91-92
Core processes, 64-66
Cross-border cooperation. *see also* AlpNet
    networks as tools for, 93-95
    trends in, 92-93
Cross-border knowledge networks. *See
    also* AlpNet